Kundalini, the divine within

BRIGITTE CALLOWAY

Illustrations by IAN CALLOWAY

YAMAS
New Zealand

Copyright © 2021 Brigitte Calloway

All rights reserved. No part of this publication may be reproduced, stored in a retrieval system or transmitted, in any form or by any means, without the prior permission of the copyright owners.

A catalog record for this book is available from the National Library of New Zealand.

ISBN: 978-0-473-58958-5
978-0-473-58959-2
978-0-473-58960-8

DEDICATION

To the most perfect people, Miriam and Amos.

CONTENTS

	Acknowledgments	i
	PREFACE	Page 1
1	KUNDALINI & SHESHA	Page 3
2	CHAKRA	Page 10
3	NADI	Page 18
4	VAYU AND GRANTHI	Page 23
5	KUNDALINI RISING	Page 27
6	KUNDALINI AND YOGA PHILOSOPHY	Page 37
7	MANTRA	Page 42
	KUNDALINI YOGA MANTRAS	Page 47
	AQUARIAN AGE MANTRAS	Page 52
	VEDIC MANTRAS	Page 56
8	MUDRA	Page 58
	MAIN MUDRAS IN KUNDALINI YOGA	Page 62
9	MEDITATION	Page 67
10	KUNDALINI YOGA	Page 71
	KUNDALINI YOGA PRANAYAMA	Page 75
	KUNDALINI YOGA ASANAS	Page 78
11	KUNDALINI YOGA KRIYAS	Page 90
	KIRTAN MEDITATION	Page 91
	SUSHMUNA MANTRA MEDITATION	Page 93

SAT KRIYA	Page 94
MEDITATION FOR DEEP SLEEP	Page 95
EGO ERADICATOR	Page 96
ARCHER KRIYA	Page 97
RELEASE STRESS KRIYA	Page 98
LAYA YOGA MEDITATION	Page 99
BEGINNER KRIYA	Page 100
ENERGISING KRIYA	Page 105
INNER SUN KRIYA	Page 109
LAYA YOGA KRIYA FOR INTUITION	Page 111
CHAKRA CLEANSING KRIYA	Page 115
KUNDALINI ACTIVATION KRIYA	Page 120
BALANCING IDA & PINGALA KRIYA	Page 125
RADIANT BODY KRIYA	Page 127
POWER KRIYA	Page 136
CLEANSING THE 8th CHAKRA KRIYA	Page 143
AURA BALANCING KRIYA	Page 147
KUNDALINI FLOW KRIYA	Page 151
MANIPURA ACTIVATION KRIYA	Page 159
KRIYA FOR STAMINA	Page 163
ADVANCED MASTER KRIYAS	Page 170
BACK FLIXIBILITY KRIYA	Page 170
ADVANCED MEDITATION	Page 174
10 MINUTES KRIYA	Page 175

	STRONG CORE KRIYA	Page 178
12	NUTRITION	Page 182
13	SADHANA	Page 186
	FROM A YOGI TO ANOTHER	Page 190
	REFERENCES	Page 195

ACKNOWLEDGMENTS

I am forever grateful to the great Sages, who discovered thousands of years ago the path that leads to the absolute light. Their wisdom and knowledge stayed strong over time and was and still is the source of enlightenment for many people searching for the same light.

I would like to thank all the yogis around the world, who inspired me and who, in good and bad times, kept me focused on my practice.

My forever gratitude goes to this large Kundalini yoga family, who like me, wakes up before sunrise only to catch the ambrosial hours and who carries on the teachings of this divine yoga by chanting, meditating and focusing on things that matter.

A huge thanks to my husband Ian, who didn't find me weird because I embraced this intense passion for Kundalini yoga and the Vedic philosophy; also for the beautiful drawings he made for this book. I owe him so much!

Special thanks to my friend Paul Copper, who made time to proofread my gibberish writing so that this book could be published.

Forever appreciation to my spiritual Lodge. We are all part of this large universal family that will exist forever!

PREFACE

Spirituality, awareness and awakening are perhaps the most discussed topics these days. In a world that proved to be fragile lately, people are searching for spirituality, when in fact we are all spiritual beings anyway. However, new paths that promise enlightenment are rapidly spreading around, replacing established religious ideas and making crowds of adepts. People want immortality guaranteed... and I am no different!

The ancient Vedic philosophy is my first love and, if I am sure about something, it is that this passion will last forever. I embarked on this journey over thirty years ago, after attending a meditation group, ran in my birth country, by some visiting Russian yogis. The group they formed included twenty people they carefully picked, with me being the youngest, just a teenager, and definitely the most opinionated of all. With their help, I have discovered the union with God and followed its light ever since. The light got brighter in time though and was perfectly revealed through the merge of Vedanta school of philosophy I adhered to and Kundalini yoga I have practiced for many years.

I have to admit that I am not a novice in Vedic philosophy, but I am not an expert either. Nobody is! The Vedic wisdom is wider than the human mind would comprehend... at least in my opinion. However, I dedicated three decades of my life to understanding and decoding the Vedas, Upanishads, Ramayana, Mahabharata, Bhagavad Gita, the Sustras, the Puranas, the Samhitas, Sri Isopanishad, Srimad Bhagavatam and many other ancient texts. Sometimes I had to translate them myself only to make sure that the right words are in the right context.

During the years, I understood that we, humans, are as divine as the concept of holiness is because God is within us in a form of an energy that encompasses a divine consciousness. I discovered that life force many years ago and I learnt to live spiritually, based on my divine nature, in a material world that has nothing to do with spirituality. I experienced myself the rise of the divine Kundalini Shakti, the eternal feminine attribute of wholeness and I absorbed aspects of this planet's beauty rather than focusing on the minuses that came with our human nature.

Kundalini yoga, also called the yoga of awareness, is sacred and its effects are out of ordinary; in most cases even inexplicable. The yoga of awakening the serpent energy has its roots in the Vedic society, thousands of years before Christ stepped on earth.

In this book, I attempt to explore some of the mysteries of Kundalini, the life force within us, as well as the phenomena of awakening the divine energy, based on the words transmitted thousands of years ago by the Rishis and on my own experiences too. I also aim to reveal some Kundalini yoga Kriyas, sacred Mantras and Mudras that helped me reach the point I am at now. This book is a product of many years of researching data about the phenomenal Kundalini Shakti and worshiping the God within.

CHAPTER 1

KUNDALINI & SHESHA

I was in my early twenties when I heard for the first time about Kundalini and for many years I tried to decode its mysteries. There weren't many writings then on the topic other than the ancient Vedic texts, so I started with them. I thought that I would master in a blink of an eye everything about the divine energy that stays dormant in every human being, but looking back now, I realise how naive I was. Thirty years later, I am still fascinated about Kundalini and yet don't know everything about it.

Every culture, religion and school of thought refers to Kundalini as the divine embodied consciousness in our frail bodies. The Bible calls it *"the tree of life"*, Islam names it *"the sweet breeze"*, whilst in Judaism and Kabbalah is Shekinah, the feminine quality of God itself. The ancient Egyptians linked it to the staff of Osiris[1]. In ancient Greece, Plato mentioned it in *"Timaeus"*, a famous dialogue aiming to explain the creation of the universe, as being *"the divine seed that resides in us"*. In Mesopotamia, its symbol was nothing else than Caduceus, the ideogram adopted by the medical system.

Even neuroscience agreed on the existence of the powerful Kundalini Shakti. The famous psychoanalyst Carl Jung[2] associated it with aspects of the unconscious dimension of the human mind, whilst some medical researchers even adopted the term of *"Kundalini syndrome"*.

But it was in the Yoga Upanishads[3] where the holy Shakti (energy) was first mentioned as a divine feminine energy, opposing to Shiva[4], the masculine aspect of our being; therefore our own human nature being based on the symbiosis Shiva or consciousness and Shakti or power. The Upanishads called the mysterious energy Kundalini, from the Sanskrit root *"kundala"* that means *"coiled"* or *"circular"*.

The Yoga Upanishads, part of the Krishna Yajurveda[5], describe the temperamental Kundalini as being coiled up since birth at the base of the spine, in Muladhara, the Root Chakra area. The Rishis[6] believed that we were born with this serpent energy, looking very similar to a snake, coiled in three and a half spirals and having a totally different consciousness than our own.

The Sages associated Yoni[7] with Kundalini Shakti and Linga[8] with Shiva or Cosmic Consciousness. Yoni is in fact the representation of the Goddess Shakti, whilst Linga is the masculine equivalent, attributed to Shiva. Therefore, together, Yoni and Linga denote the unity of the microcosm and macrocosm or of Creation and Creator. In this wholeness, Kundalini is the gateway to enlightenment.

The Sages were very specific about the role played by Kundalini energy, placed in us from the very first moment we came to this planet. They believed that enlightenment and awakening cannot exist in the absence of Shakti being aroused and that, once this happens, we are able to totally understand the concept of Brahman, the Ultimate Reality, the source of creation of all that is.

Because they were the first to bring Kundalini in the limelight, the Rishis explained in details how this amazing force could be released from its seat, placed in the Muladhara Chakra area. They identified seven energetic centers they called Cakra (or Chakra) and three main Nadis (energy vessels), Ida Pingala and Sushumna. They explained how, when agitated, Kundalini snake leaves its burrow and travels in Sushumna, piercing one by one each Chakra, up to Sahasrara, the thousand petals chakra at the crown of the head, in a process called Shakti Chalana[9]. This is the moment when we realise the union of Atman, the Universal Self, with Brahman[10], the Cosmic Consciousness. This is the awakening every religion, mystical and philosophical school talks about and this is the giant step towards Moksha[11], the spiritual liberation, required in breaking Samsara[12], the cycle of reincarnations. This aspect, defined as Laya[13] or the dissolution of the human ego and absorption into the cosmic dimension, is in fact the sole purpose of each brand of yoga.

However, of all traditional yoga schools, Kundalini yoga deals mostly with the aspect of Kundalini, blending in perfectly the features of Bhakti (devotion), Raja (meditation) and Shakti (expression of mental power or control).

Kundalini yoga Kriyas (sequences) are a symbiosis of powerful Mantras, precise successions of Asanas (postures), Pranayama (breathing technique) and meditation procedures that would take a yogi to dissolving the Self and be one with the cosmic reality. Therefore, it accomplishes the purpose of four types of yoga, Mantra yoga[14], Hatha yoga[15], Laya yoga[16] and Raja yoga[17], that lead to arousing the Kundalini energy as described in the Shiva

Samhita[18].

Kundalini yogis all around the world argue that awakening the spiritual life force within would help them realise their life purpose and break aspects of their own karma, so there is no doubt that, as a Kundalini yogi myself, I find the serpent energy essential in my own life path. For me, Kundalini yoga is the pilgrimage I started long time ago and ultimately ended up reaching the point I dreamt about when I first heard about Kundalini in my early twenties.

The Eastern world accepts things without worrying too much about why they are the way they are, whilst the Western society is much more pragmatic. For the Westerner, who consents on the existence of organs, muscles and tissues in the human body just because they can be revealed in an ultrasound or MRI scan, the fact that energy could stay latent at the base of the spine is a misconception of the daily reality. So, the question that arises is related to the source of this energy. Well, the answer is obvious really: matter and energy are related. Matter as we know it is just another form of energy. Again, the Vedas[19] hold the answer to many of the controversial subjects for science whilst crystal clear for quantum physics.

The Vedas initiated the idea that Agni[20], translated as *"fire"*, but associated with the word *"energy"*, is the source of all creation. Aiteraya Brahmana[21], part of Rigveda[22], states that *"energy involves entire material creation"* (6.1.2.28). It is in this Brahmana[23] where Agni as energy is explained as devouring its parents, whom in fact represent nothing else than matter. Therefore, each creational act of material objects started from Agni as energy. So, if everything is a form of energy, matter is too. To understand this argument, I would have to start with how creation of this universe was perceived from the Vedic perspective.

Many people miss the point and get themselves lost in details when they read the Hindu cosmology myths. For instance, Vishnu[24], in the ocean, dreaming about creating the world and Brahma[25] appearing from a lotus, popping out on Vishnu's navel, has nothing to do with the two deities of Trimurti[26] creating the universe, nor with oceans and lotuses. In fact, Vishnu in the ocean symbolises the consciousness of the universe in a passive or unmanifested form, whilst Brahma is the process that started the manifested aspect of creation.

There is though another element in this myth, usually omitted or just ignored. The legend mentions Ananta Sheshanaga[27], which comes from the Adi Shesha or *"the first Shesha"* and Ananta Shesha or *"the endless Shesha"*. It is said that Shesha floats on the ocean, forming Vishnu's bed.

Shesha is symbolised by a kind of snake; when the snake uncoils forward, creation starts, whilst when it uncoils backward, the universe is dissolved. Therefore, Shesha is a manifestation of everything possible in the universe, whilst Naga[28] refers to the semi-divine race, formed by divine and serpent half human race, which it is believed that can take human forms too. So, the whole universe started from the synergy of divine consciousness and the serpent energy implanted in humans with Naga characteristics.

Shesha's name goes back to the Sanskrit root *"sis"*, which means *"something that remains from beginning to end"*. That would perhaps connect Shesha with one of the five elements the Vedas mention, ether, which existed before creation. If Shesha snake, which resemble the Kundalini ideogram or the infinity symbol, was there even before the universe was manifested, something must have happened to initiate the creation.

The Rishis believed that the source of creation was Brahmanda

Vishphotak, term known these days as the Big Bang. Thus, creation was ignited by a spark of energy that led to Panchikaranam[29] (from *"Panch"* that means *"five"* and *"Karanam"* meaning *"the act of"*) or the manifestation of matter as five elements: Tejas (fire), Vayu (wind), Prithvi (earth), Apah (water) and Akash (ether). This violent spark initiated the explosion necessary for matter as another form of energy to manifest, so it is just fair to wonder if the divine force was there from the beginning of times.

Well, to be perfectly honest, the Big Bang was not the beginning! It was the serpent Adi Shesha, or the original Shesha, the serpent energetic field that allowed creation to begin from the Black Hole. Therefore, Shesha is known as Nagaraja or the supremacy of all Naga of primary beings. This is the point when Brahman, the Cosmic Reality, expanded. Brahman comes from the Sanskrit root *"brh"* meaning *"to expand or to promote"* and implies the only metaphysical concept that cannot be explained or comprehended by the human mind.

The Vedas describe Atman, the Self, as being identical with Brahman; therefore Saguna Brahman[30] being part of Nirguna Brahman[31]. Saguna and Nirguna are just two different ways of relating to Brahman, the absoluteness. Whilst Saguna perceives Brahman beyond time and space, Nirguna associates a form or an identity to it, which is never constant by the way. Different schools of Vedic philosophy relate Brahman to either Saguna or Nirguna; however they all agree that Brahman is the Absolute Reality.

Vedanta philosophy argues that the universe is Brahman as much as it is Atman too. But for us, Kundalini yogis, this initiates the thought that the divine spark of the Cosmic Consciousness is within us.

Is this flicker Kundalini Shakti in a shape of a snake half asleep in the Muladhara Chakra area, or the Shesha that allows the raise of consciousness to occur and manifest, I would ask myself. Well, for me, the answer is both! Therefore, I would argue that Kundalini was part of the energy released in the original creation act and that, once awakened and reaching Sahasrara, the thousand petals Crown Chakra, the cycle is complete with the energy being released back to the universe.

CHAPTER 2

CHAKRA

The ancient Vedic Sages were the first to reveal the energetic centers in the human body they called Cakra or Chakra and ever since, the Western world adopted them and re-defined them to suit modern faiths and beliefs. New Age movements used them in holistic practices whilst theosophists as CW Leadbeater[32] described insights of the topic, based on his own meditations.

With every attempt to understand them, the seven Chakras described by the Rishis became one hundred and fourteen major, minor and advanced energetic organs. The truth is though that the Sages talked about seven major Chakras only, situated in straight line from the tail bone to the top of the head, never relating them to feelings and emotions as the modern world tends to do. They perceived some of these organs of energy as having very complex structures, with other Chakras, Bindus (points), spheres and rings of energy within.

The Chakras are usually viewed as wheels of energy. In fact, translated from Sanskrit, the word has many meanings: a disc, a ring and even the shape of the moon and the sun. If in the

microcosm represented by the human body, the Chakras relate to wheels of energy or vortexes, in the macrocosm of the universe, the same wheels are linked to creation (Srishti Chakra), to life of the planet (Jivana Chakra) or to time (Kala Chakra); Brahman as a wheel (Brahman Chakra) overseeing the whole Rti (order of the universe).

The Yoga Upanishads are the main texts that describe in detail the main seven Chakras, pierced by Kundalini Shakti on the way towards enlightenment. These Upanishads[33] state that each Chakra is a centre of Prana Shakti (vital force) and each represents a different level of consciousness based on its placement and activation of physical, emotional or spiritual energies involved. The Rishis identified the energy wheels as lotus flowers and attributed each Chakra a certain number of lotus petals, according to the numbers of Nadi (energy vessels) that cross them.

The first Chakra, located at the base of the spine is Muladhara or the Root Chakra, which has four petals and is associated with the colour yellow. In early representations, this vortex of energy has often the symbol of a square. Muladhara represents the earthy energy that grounds us. This is the seat of Kundalini Shakti and this is where its journey of awakening and rising towards the crown starts.

The Rishis said that in this wheel of energy, there is a Yoni and within it, a great Linga. Muladhara is also the seat of Samskara or the imprint of potential karma. The Root Chakra is represented by the sacred syllable LAM. The Vedic texts associate Muladhara to Brahma, the Creator, the root of all matter and existence.

The second Chakra is Svadhishthana or the Sacral Chakra, situated about two fingers above Muladhara, being considered the seat of existence. In fact this wheel is linked to unconscious and emotions. Svadhishthana is the space where Samskara, the potential karma, finds its expression. Also called Medhra Chakra in the later Upanishads, Svadhishthana has six petals and it relates to the element water. It is represented by the syllable VAM. In the Vedic writings, Svadhishthana is linked to Vishnu, the Sustainer of the universe, the deity often represented with blue skin and four arms.

Manipura or the Solar Plexus Chakra, symbolised by ten petals and represented by a red triangle, is the centre of digestion and metabolism. Translated from Sanskrit, Manipura means *"lustrous gem"*. In the Vedic tradition, Manipura is also called Manipuraka or Nabhi Chakra. The element associated with it is fire; therefore this is the wheel of power and action. The syllable linked to Manipura is RAM and the deity associated to it is Rudhra, the warrior, or Agni, the fire.

Anahata or the Heart Chakra, which means *"unbeaten"*, is symbolised by a lotus flower with twelve green petals. This is the centre of equilibrium, feelings and emotions. Anahata is situated in the Kshetram, the holy place in the body, near the heart. The symbol linked to Anahata is Shatkona, the six pointed star formed by intersecting two triangles, a symbol used in Yantras to prove the symbiosis of masculine and feminine. The deity associated with it is Shiva, the Destroyer, and the element linked to it is air. Anahata is represented by the syllable YAM.

Vishuddha or the Throat Chakra is the centre of sacred speech and is represented by a transparent circle, sign of Akasha (ether), with sixteen petals. Translated from Sanskrit, Vishuddha means *"especially pure"*. The element associated with it is space (ether) and the deity is the transgender form of Shiva, half man and half woman. The sacred syllable linked to Vishuddha is HAM. In the Upanishads, it is also known as Kantha Chakra or Vishuddhi.

Ajna, the Third Eye Chakra or the Eye of Shiva, is located between the eyebrows. It has two petals and it is not associated to any element or deity. In most representations, the symbol of Ajna is a transparent spiral. Because this Chakra is linked to the Pineal gland, it is the centre of psychic abilities and intuition. The Pineal gland produces melatonin, a hormone in charge with the state of falling asleep and waking up. Symbolically, Ajna does the same, being in control with awareness and spiritual awakening. Translated from Sanskrit, Ajna means *"to perceive"*. The syllable linked to Ajna is OM, same Bija (seed) associated to Sahasrara.

Sahasrara, the Crown Chakra or the thousand petals Chakra, located on the crown of the head, is the place where individuality is lost and infinity is gained. In esoteric astrology, one thousand is the number of eternity. The ideogram of this powerful wheel of energy is a lotus flower with a thousand petals, having an upward triangle in the middle. Like Ajna, Sahasrara is not linked to any element or deity. Sahasrara is the seat of Prajnanam, the highest intelligence, and the final destination of Kundalini energy. In the Vedic texts, Sahasrara is also known as Akasha Chakra, Wyomambuja or Kapalasamputa, whilst in Agni yoga[34], the doctrine started by Helena and Nicholas Roerich, as Brahmarandhra.

The first three Chakras, Muladhara, Svadhishthana and Manipura, form the Lower Triangle, the physicality of the material world, which can be associated to Bhur, the physical realm. Anahata could be linked to Bhuvah, the life force reality, whilst Vishuddha, Ajna and Sahasrara form the Higher Triangle associated to Swah, the spiritual realm, where the soul feels at home. The three realms, Bhur, Bhuvah and Swah are mentioned in the most famous Mantra, the Gayatri Mantra[35], composed around 3,500BC and included in the Rigveda.

The divine syllables linked to each Chakra form the Bija (seed) Mantra connected to specific sounds or vibrations of each of the wheels of energy. Chanting them would result in balancing the Chakras.

Understanding the seven main Chakras in the human body as described by the Rishis is primordial in mastering Kundalini awakening. However, each Chakra is so much more than just a wheel of energy in itself; each including within a whole system of mini Chakras, crossed by Nadis and points of energy.

Sahasrara is the most complex of all. It starts with the Guru Chakra, described in the Gheranda Samhita[36] (6.9), fourteen Sanskrit Hatha Yoga manuscripts: *"There is a twelve petal lotus connected with the pericarp of Sahasrara"*.

In the highest part of Sahasrara, there is the Supreme Bindu, the so-called *"dot in the circle or in the lotus"* which makes the connection with the cosmic energy, the whole. In between Guru Chakra and the Supreme Bindu[37], there is Nirvana Chakra[38], which is known as *"the hundred petals Chakra"*.

The Vedic Laya yoga mentions Ama Kala[39] with the Supreme Bindu within in the highest structure of Sahasrara. This is the point of absoluteness and oneness. The state of absorption is attempted however in the Nirvana Kala[40], where the last stage of Samadhi[41], the total dissolution and absorption, is achieved.

The reason I mentioned the complex structure of Sahasrara is because, in my opinion, most people are able to bring the temperamental Kundalini up to Ajna. The hard work starts when directing it upwards to Sahasrara.

The Western world sees Chakras as simple symbols, wheels of energy, represented by colours or lotus petals, but in the Eastern philosophy they are vessels to enlightenment. However, each Chakra is an organ with a very complicated structure, documented in the Vedic ancient texts.

Therefore, yoga is beyond a fitness movement. Yoga's purpose is the union with the universal force, achieved through practices using the levels of consciousness called Chakras. Yoga bases its tradition and philosophy on dissolution of ego and self and absorption into the highest realm. In my opinion, Kundalini yoga achieves exactly that. As simple as it may be perceived by the Western world, Kundalini yoga uses levels of meditation that are very profound, dissolution being perhaps reached through the symbiosis of Asanas, visualization and sound.

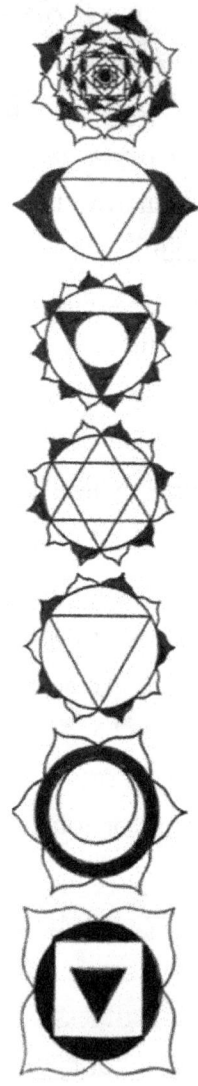

Sacred Mantras in conjunction with Mudras, gestures that seal energy, are each Kundalini yogi's forte. Therefore, through Kundalini yoga, the yogi is in charge with agitating the Shakti, bringing it up to the divine Sahasrara and making the connection with the wholeness.

The Mother energy, Kundalini or Adi Shakti, is the Cosmic power we all have within us, the only mystic force that can lead us to the ultimate truth, as described in Rigveda (I.89.10): *"The Primal Light (Adi Shakti) is the abode of the Celestial; the Primal Light is Space; the Primal Light is Mother, Father and the Son. The Primal Light is the Universal Deities; the Primal Light is the Five Races of Mortals; the Primal Light is all that has and will be born"*.

CHAPTER 3

NADI

Nadis are energy vessels or nerves in the human body. Translated from Sanskrit, Nadi means *"river"* or *"what flows and makes sound"*. In the Rigveda, the holy rivers are the only ones that flow directly into a sea. In the same way, the most important Nadis in the body are the ones in charge directly with the flow of Kundalini Shakti.

Chandogya Upanishad[42] 8.6.6 mentions one hundred and one Nadis starting from the heart out. *"In the heart, there is Jivatma (life force). Here a hundred and one Nadis arise. For each of these Nadis, there are one hundred Nadikas (small nadis). For each of these, there are thousands more. In these, Vyana moves"*. Vyana Vayu (wind) brings balance in the body and is in charge with the functioning of the muscular system.

Same number appears in Katha Upanishad[43] (6.16): *"There are a hundred and one vessels of the heart and the chief of them pierces through the head. By that one going upwards, he obtains deathlessness. The others are for the purpose of carrying the soul to diverse other Lokas"*. This text states that with the flow of the primal energy upward, one reaches the cosmic identity. The Lokas[44] refer to the different planes of existence or worlds in Vedic philosophy.

It is said that there are seventy-two thousand Nadis in the human body. However the primordial Nadis are: Ida, Pingala and Sushumna. Kshurika Upanishad[45], part of Atharveda[46] describes them clearly: *"Where on the left guards Ida and on the right the Pingala. Between them is a chief spot. He who knows it, knows the Veda. Dustless, entering into Brahman, the Sushumna is related to it. It's the pillow on which rest the 72,000 arteries"* (16.175).

Ida means *"comfort"* and it directs energy with a cooling effect associated with the lunar, passive feminine aspect. It starts in the left side of the body and travels towards the left nostril. Ida governs the processes of thinking, emotions in general and all the functions of the mind linked to intelligence.

Pingala, which means *"orange"*, runs on the right side of the body traveling towards the right nostril. It is also known as *"the Channel of the Sun"* because it is linked to the solar, active masculine principle and its effect is a heating energy. Pingala governs will, power and creative abilities.

Ida and Pingala form a caduceus, crisscrossing around Sushumna, the main Prana (vital energy) vessel in the human body. Sushumna, or Sukha Mana (Sukta means *"joyful"* and Mana means *"mind"*), connects Muladhara with Sahasrara, going in the middle of the spinal cord, and is the channel in which Kundalini Shakti travels. Sushumna is also known as Sunya, Mahapatha and Pradavi and is associated with the Astral Body.

Ida, Pingala and Sushumna meet in Ajna, where they form Mukta Triveni or *"the Threefold Knot of Liberation"*. Translated from Sanskrit, Mukta means *"liberating"* and Triveni means *"braided"*. Similarly, their junction in Muladhara Chakra is called Yukta Triveni. Translated from Sanskrit, Yukta means *"united"*.

The Vedic texts mention three more Nadis within Sushumna: Vajra, Brahma and Chitrini. Kundalini energy travels through these too.

Brahma Nadi, also known as Brahmarandhra, means *"divine"* and lies within Chitrini Nadi. When Kundalini travels through Brahma Nadi, it absorbs all cosmic principles.

Chitrini Nadi or Chitra is within Vajra Nadi, which means *"firmness"*. Chitrini has an opening named Brahmadvara or *"the door of Brahman"*. This is the channel Kundalini passes through when awakened on the way to Kula Marga[47] or the Royal Path. Therefore, Chitrini is considered the seed of all spiritual abilities.

What I have noticed during the years I researched the Vedic writings and practiced Kundalini yoga is that things are straightforward in yoga. There is never anything new to be invented and the simplest things are usually the ones that are right. Similarly, Kundalini yoga Kriyas are set in stone and any change to them would stay against a yogi's goals. They are simple and complex in the same time.

The entire process of awakening the Shakti starts with healthy, unblocked Nadis. The whole science of Kundalini begins with that, so there is no doubt why Nadis are so well documented in the Vedic texts. The procedure itself is simple and it consists in alternate nostril breathing.

There should be an equilibrium of feminine and masculine in each being; too much or not enough of one can create chaos in the physical body. Therefore, through one nostril breathing, one can identify the dominant nostril and the dominant side of their body and through alternate nostrils breathing, one is able to regulate the flow.

There are breathing techniques in yoga that can cool down or heat up the body. Therefore, if Ida is dominant as too much cooling occurs, a Pranayama that would heat up the body can be performed. And to be perfectly honest, there are many to choose from. In a similar way, if Pingala brings too much heating, a cooling Pranayama can always be executed. However, I believe that Nadi Shodana (alternate nostril breathing) is always the starting point and may be more than enough to bring back the equilibrium. Our Sages performed it thousands of years ago and nowadays it has the same effect.

Nadi Shodana has its root in Nadi Shuddhi, which means *"removing the impurities in the Nadis"*. Its effect is detoxification and purification. Even outside of the practice of Kundalini rising, the alternate nostril breathing is beneficial for everybody and, if performed correctly, it regulates the temperature of the body and it calms down the mind.

CHAPTER 4

VAYU AND GRANTHI

Everything in the universe vibrates. Therefore everything within us is based on vibration too.

Prana, the essential energy that keeps us alive, flows in the body in seventy-two strings that act as meridians, controlled by the three central channels Ida, Pingala and Sushumna. As the Chakras vibrate, the seventy-two strings vibrate too in seventy-two thousand channels, carrying energy. In yoga, the perfect vibration is achieved through the symbiosis Shakti and Bhakti. Shakti is the energy involved in repetition, which in time creates precision, and Bhakti is accepting and surrendering in devotion.

Now that we have an idea about how Chakras and Nadis move the energy in our bodies, there is primordial to understand what is the structure that pushes energy through these organs. Well, these forces are called Vayus or *"winds"*.

The Sages talked about forty-nine Vayus, the main five being used in each branch of yoga. These are Prana Vayu, Apana Vayu, Vyana Vayu, Udana Vayu and Samana Vayu. These five winds push the energy upward and downward creating the balance in the human body.

Prana Vayu, situated in the heart area means *"moving forward air"*, therefore creates a flow of energy inward and upward. This energy nourishes the brain and the eyes.

The second wind is Apana Vayu, which means *"the air that moves away"*. It is situated in the pelvic area and creates the flow of energy downward and out installing balance in the kidneys area and urinary tracts.

Vyana Vayu means *"outward moving air"* and is situated in the chest area. Its role is moving the energy from the centre of the body to the periphery and is in charge with blood circulation.

Udana Vayu means *"that which carries upward"* and works the energy in a circular flow around the neck and head. It is situated in the throat area and regulates the flow from the heart area to the head, activating the five main senses.

Samana Vayu means *"the balancing air"* and flows from the periphery towards the center of the body. This wind regulates digestion.

If Prana, the vital force, divides itself in five winds, controlling different parts of the body and creating equilibrium in the body, the way its flow can be controlled is through Pranayama or breathing, which is considered one of the eight limbs of yoga. There are also certain Asanas that can improve the energy flow.

Kundalini Yoga Upanishad mentions the Vayus pushing Kundalini on the way to Sahasrara, also describing the manner each stirs the divine Shakti. However, on its travel upwards, Kundalini would meet three Granthi (knots), also described in the same Upanishad and well known by the yogic community.

Granthis are bundles of Nadis that stop Kundalini energy entering or travelling in Sushumna. Yogis consider these energy knots as being blocks of personality that prevent the flow of Prana in the body.

The first knot Kundalini has to pierce is Brahmna Granthi, situated between Muladhara and Svadhishthana. It is also called *"the perineal knot"* and it is linked to fear. Next is Vishnu Granthi, also called *"the navel knot"*. It is situated between Manipura and Anahata and it is linked to ego. Once this is overcome, Kundalini faces the third knot, called Rudra Granthi or *"the forehead knot"*, situated between Anahata and Ajna. Also called Shiva Granthi, this energetic knot is linked to emotional attachment.

The yogic tradition starting in the Vedas teaches that all three Granthis can be untied using Bandhas, which lock Prana in different areas. Bandhas are body locks that help shaping the pattern of energy.

Brahma Granthi can be untied if Mula Bandha or the *"Root Bandha"* is performed in a very simple manner by contracting the pelvic floor. Once released because of the pressure created, Vayu will blow Kundalini upward. *"Apana (breath), which has an downward tendency, is forced up by the sphincter muscles of the anus. Mula Bandha is the name of this process"* (Kundalini Yoga Upanishad 36).

Vishnu Granthi can be untied when performing Uddiyana Bandha by holding the breath whilst pressing the abdominal wall inward. *"At the end of the Kunbhaka (breath retention) and at the beginning of expiration, Uddiyana Bandha should be performed. Because Prana Uddiyate, or the Prana, goes up the Sushumna in this Bandha, the Yogis call it Uddiyana"* (Kundalini Yoga Upanishad 40).

Finally, Rudra Granthi can be unblocked when engaging Jalandhara Bandha, also called *"the chin lock"*, by bringing the chin in the chest. *"This should be practiced at the end of Puraka (after inhalation). This is of the form of contraction of the neck and is an impediment to the passage of Vayu upwards"* (Kundalini Yoga Upanishad 42)

An experienced yogi would know how to inhale and exhale, also how and when to retain their breath whilst performing the Bandhas. Practice and perseverance is needed in order to master the locks of energy, but in yoga everything is possible; and when all three locks are performed naturally and comfortably, another Bandha can be introduced. It is called Maha Bandha and incorporates all three Mula, Uddiyana and Jalandhara Bandhas simultaneously.

CHAPTER 5

KUNDALINI RISING

Some people may believe that Kundalini yoga is the only practice that help one raising the divine energy from Muladhara to Sahasrara and experience the union with the Absolute Reality. I would however disagree. During the years, I came across people who went through traumatic events that had led to possible Kundalini awakenings. I am not sure if anybody can argue that there is only one cause that can initiate one effect only.

Some people may wonder if Kundalini awakening is important and if every single person searching for enlightenment should experience it. I don't hold the answer unfortunately. It may or it may not be important. It was for me though!

The Internet is full of Kundalini awakening episodes, one more orgasmic than the other, so there is no doubt why many people would ask themselves if they would really be prepared to experience something so dramatic. Well, the seven spindles of energy called Chakras are in fact levels of consciousness one should aim to reach on the path towards spiritual awakening. In my opinion, they can be achieved in meditation. *"Silence is the language of God"* is one of the main sayings in Vedanta[48] school of Vedic philosophy. Therefore, awareness and contemplation are the keys in realising the oneness with the cosmos.

Passing through the mental stages of the first six Chakras would help one perceiving the reality beyond the material world; reaching a higher consciousness through Sahasrara would create the union yoga aims for. This is the state of non-duality, where the soul recognises itself as being one with the universe.

To define the two stages of Kundalini, awakening and arousing, my suggestion is understanding first the concept of consciousness. My perspective comes again from Vedanta philosophy I embraced many years ago.

We are conscious beings; therefore we cannot dissociate ourselves from our own consciousness. However, we cannot define consciousness as being a quality of our minds, because in fact consciousness is a witness of our Vritti[49], the mental activity of our own minds. Therefore, we are our own consciousness. The modern society taught us otherwise though. From early stages in our lives, we learnt to identify ourselves with our body, gender, level of intelligence, skills and abilities. The truth is that consciousness is the simple *"I am"*, not linked to any physical dimension of our own being. We may live in a material world, which we contemplate and absorb in through our senses, but we are spiritual beings, aiming to reach the oneness potential we all have within us.

Vedanta acknowledges the veil of ignorance we all surround ourselves with and calls it Maya[50], illusion. This veil permits us to know that we are conscious beings whilst ignoring the extraordinary source of our essence. We live in our Lower Triangle of the materialistic Chakras, Muladhara, Svadhishthana and Manipura, not allowing ourselves to raise our awareness to higher levels.

The good news is that we cannot possess or lose consciousness. We are it. Therefore, through awareness we can lift the veil of ignorance and become the observer of the absolute reality. This is exactly what Kundalini awakening is about. It is the realisation that *"I am"* is our true identity and that there is no need to see ourselves outside of the *"I-ness"*. Therefore, Kundalini awakening is the first step towards spirituality; a giant move from what is not important to what it really matters. The arousal of the divine Shakti is achieved only when we allow raising our levels of consciousness.

Mandukya Upanishad[51], part of Atharveda, describes the four different perspectives of the world based on the four Avasthas or levels of consciousness. In Jagrut or the waking state, the individual, called Vaisvanasa, observes the world; each object perceived being a separate entity from their own Jiva (being). Vaisvanasa is a Sanskrit term meaning *"related to Visvanara"*, a concept having its roots in the Universal Cosmic Man (*"Vishva"* means *"universe"* and *"Narah"* means *"Cosmic Man"*).

In Swapna, or the inward cognitive state of dreaming, the being is called Taijasa, which means *"one who is bright"*. The opening to the soul consciousness is achieved however in Sushupti or the dreamless sleep, in which the being is called Prajna or *"the one who is able to understand"*.

Chandogya Upanishad, part of Samaveda[52], describes these three states of consciousness, linking them to the body itself, in a concept called *"The Three Bodies Doctrine"*[53]. According to it, the waking state is associated with the gross body, the dreaming state is linked to the subtle body and the state of deep sleep to the casual body. The gross body is purely physical; the subtle body is neither physical nor spiritual, whilst the casual body originates in Avidya (ignorance).

Above these three levels, there is Turiya[54], the fourth state that is the highest consciousness, neither inward, nor outward cognitive. This is the state of understanding the Supreme Reality defined as Brahman. Turiya, which means *"the fourth"*, is related to the fourth level of consciousness that is the highest state a being is able to achieve, mentioned in Mandukya Upanishad 7 as *"being one with the Self, cessation of development, tranquil, benign, without a second, such they think is the fourth. He is the Self (Atman). He should be discerned"*. Therefore, if Kundalini awakening comes from self-realisation, rising Shakti reaching Sahasrara is the state of Turiya.

In reaching Turiya, the obstacle is the veil of ignorance created by the Koshas[55]. Translated from Sanskrit, Koshas mean *"sheaths"* and are in fact layers over the subtle body. Taittiriya Upanishad[56] identifies five Koshas.

The first is Annamaya Kosha, in which beings are identifying themselves with the object of the body that is not eternal, therefore mortal.

Pranamaya Kosha is the layer of our vital force Prana. Our bodies function because of Prana. Manomaya Kosha is formed by our minds and sensory organs that observe, analyse and separate between the *"I"* and the rest.

Vijnanamaya Kosha is the layer of our intellectual faculties with whatever knowledge we acquire. Knowledge is not unchangeable, therefore not constant either.

Anandamaya Kosha is the state of pure bliss and is mostly achieved during deep sleep. Because it wasn't fully present in the waking state, the ultimate realisation is that the only bliss is our divine nature, given by the fact that our Self is the only reality.

The structure of our human nature is complex and we make it sound even more complicated. In fact, all we are is our divine nature. Everything outside the *"I-ness"* is Maya or illusion.

Kundalini rising is the practice that brings us back to the real seed of our soul. Therefore, the awakening of the phenomenal Shakti placed in us before birth, can be an effect of a spiritual practice, a dramatic event or just the evolution of our consciousness. With each step of evolvement, one of the Chakras is pierced, a block is untied and a veil is lifted. It may take time to realise that the material world is not our true identity and it may need practice and determination to live according to the Kundalini consciousness placed in us.

The Vedic texts affirm that the change from physical to spiritual can occur in a practice called yoga. If you take this literally, you would think that you have to begin stretching, get more physical and perform Asanas out of the ordinary. In fact, yoga means more than that. Yoga is the union one can achieve with the universe, with the Cosmic Soul; call it God by every name invented by religious dogmas. Yoga is the supreme state of consciousness; also Kundalini energy reaching Sahasrara. I would therefore mention the two ways of achieving Kundalini awakening as described by the Vedic Sages, not denying though that there may be other methods too.

The first practice described is Shaktipat, the ceremonial of initiation, in which a master or a guru transmits spiritual energy to a student. Guru means exactly that. *"Gu"* is *"dark"* and *"Ru"* is *"light"*; therefore the origin of the word *"mentor"* is bringing one from darkness to light.

Shaktipat has its origin in ancient times and, since then it was performed as an initiation into the Kula or the world spiritual family. In this ritual, Mantras play a primordial role, but I witnessed masters using the power of touch instead.

Some people believe that Shaktipat has an immediate result, but this is not always the case because there are usually seven levels of intensity involved. Therefore, the effect can be instant or magnified in time according to how prepared to surrender the student is and how ideal the guru is for them. Like everything else in the world, Shaktipat is about the perfect symbiosis of student and mentor, a relationship in which both have to accept, surrender and trust.

Since the ancient pre-Vedic times, Shaktipat is still practiced in many parts of the world and there is no doubt why. We all need mentors, people more evolved than us, people who can help us reaching our spiritual goals faster. However, the only question arising is how important are the spiritual experiences and, if they are, are they the only ones that matter?

To be perfectly honest, the climax of a spiritual event is far beyond the level of spirituality achieved in time through self-realisation. Advaita Vedanta[57], a non-dualistic school of Vedanta philosophy, associates reaching Samadhi with the state of self-realisation. Samadhi is in fact the meditative consciousness, a state that enable achieving the dissolution of self and reaching absorption. This concept is described in the Maitrayaniya Upanishad[58], part of Yajurveda[59].

The *"Yoga Sutras of Patanjali"*[60] also describe the stages necessary in reaching Samadhi. The first degree is Dharana or concentration. In this level, the mind has to be aware of the object of concentration, from infiniteness to the limited space.

The next extent is Vyasa or the focus on one point in the body, in most cases the Third Eye, the point situated in between the eyebrows, allowing the mind to ignore any other detail. The same procedure is followed in every meditation in Kundalini yoga.

I don't deny the importance of having mentors or gurus, experienced and knowledgeable enlightened people who can help one step on the path of spirituality and enlightenment. With the power of touch, sound or thought, they can help a student learn the steps desired in reaching Samadhi. What I would argue though is that this may not be the only way.

Kundalini Yoga Upanishad[61] describes the rising of the divine Shakti as a process that takes time. *"With the mind firmly fixed on the Truth, the practice of Pranayama should be performed daily. Then the mind takes its response in the Sushumna"* (verse 56).

The practice of arousing Kundalini described in this Upanishad is based on Pranayama, Bandhas, Mantras and the science of Khechari Vidya. The text says that *"the key to this science is kept a profound secret. The secret is revealed by adepts only at initiation"*. Therefore, as much as one tries to reach wholeness, mentorship is paramount.

Kundalini awakening cannot be achieved randomly and cannot be learnt by acquiring knowledge from books or Internet, so in a way or another, the Shaktipat initiation will always play a role even if not in the traditional way.

The self-proclaimed guru is not the guru the Rishis talked about. They believed that one who can teach the Divine yoga is the true guru. As an analogy, Kundalini yoga proclaims that each student is a guru in making, so the yoga science the Sages referred to will always be transmitted from one mentor to the one in formation.

In order to understand what really happens in the process of

Kundalini awakening, I propose to go back to the roots, to Kundalini Yoga Upanishad and to the description made by the Sages. They said that the only way to awake the dormant Kundalini is by agitating it. As a modern analogy, I would suggest to imagine the effect produced by shaking a champagne bottle. The pressure produced in the bottle would ignite the rest. Same with Kundalini…

The Sages said that the restrain of Prana or breath and Sarasvati Chalana would force the snake to uncoil. Sarasvati or Arundati is a Nadi situated in the West of the navel where Kundalini has to travel first. Kundalini will stay perfectly erect when we first inhale. There is however something to be mentioned about breathing too.

The yoga texts teach us the difference in units or digits of air between breathing in and breathing out. A normal person breathes in twelve units of air and exhales sixteen. Therefore with each cycle of inhaling and exhaling, we lose four units of Prana. There is no doubt why we, modern people, feel so exhausted at the end of the day!

For Kundalini Shakti to straighten and start traveling toward Chakras, inhaling and exhaling have to be at the same capacity of sixteen units. Then, by holding firm the ribs with the forefingers and thumbs of both hands, Kundalini gets agitated and enters into Sushumna, alongside the units of Prana, which will create furthermore pressure.

On the way upwards, after engaging Mula Bandha, the first lock, Kundalini pierces Svadhishthana, then Manipura, untying the first two Granthis too. After locking the Uddiyana Bandha, Shakti pierces Anahata and gets closer to Vishuddha and, once Jalandhara Bandha is executed, it goes through the Throat Chakra. Pushing the energy towards Ajna involves the Kechari Mudra, which is performed with the tongue that touches the pressure point just beneath the Pineal gland. Once this gland is activated, Kundalini pierces Ajna.

As I have said, it may be easy to bring the temperamental feminine energy to the Third Eye and difficult to push it further. However, when it reaches Sahasrara, Kundalini Shakti has to travel through its very complicated structure, starting with the Mandala (sphere) of the moon, then of the sun.

Reaching the centre of Sahasrara, the energy gives up the human dimensions, materialised by the *"eight forms of Prakriti: earth, water, fire, air, ether, mind intellect and egoism"* and dissolves itself in the Supreme Bindu, in Sahasrara. Leaving its initial state behind, Kundalini becomes Shakhini[62], the Mother Earth, still having three and a half coils.

Samani (dissolution) starts in the moment Shakhini wraps a first coil around the Supreme Bindu and the next two around the Nada and the Shakti. The absorption happens when the last half coil of Shakhini is sucked up in Parama Shiva, the higher aspect of consciousness. This is the state of Samadhi.

Kundalini Yoga Upanishad describes this moment as *"by causing the body made of the elements to be absorbed in the subtle state, in a form of the Paramatman or the supreme Deity, the body of the yogi gives up its impure corporal state"*.

Dissolution is a state everybody can achieve. Some will, others won't. However, if I would have to define it, I would name it as the fifth level of consciousness or perhaps the transcendence into the fifth reality. It is the state where everything comes together and the union of Shiva as consciousness and Shakti as power when the essence of all is finally achieved. It is also the level of harmony of polarities, masculine and feminine, united with the energy of the universe; but most of all it is the realm we are meant to live in.

From an esoteric point of view, the Chakras are degrees of consciousness. Therefore the physical procedure described by the Rishis is achievable, in my opinion, through spiritual evolvement. Once one leaves behind the physicality of this world, the materialism and the egoism, one by one the Chakras are pierced, blocks of energy are overcome and the divine consciousness starts its travel toward the upper levels.

It takes dedication, practice, selflessness and awareness of what is important. We cannot buy spirituality, but we can definitely shift the awareness and raise our consciousness. Having a divine nature is more a responsibility than a privilege!

CHAPTER 6

KUNDALINI AND YOGA PHILOSOPHY

We link the concept of Kundalini to Chakras as energy organs in the body, omitting the fact that Chakras are in fact centers of spiritual and psychic powers, able to shift the consciousness to higher realms. Therefore, Kundalini itself is the superconscious extent of our own consciousness we are meant to reach in our evolution on this planet.

To understand the phenomena of Kundalini, we would however have to go back in time and acknowledge the role played by yoga philosophy, starting in the ancient mysterious times up to this very moment.

The Vedic system admits six Darshans (schools) of philosophy (Nyana, Vaisheshika, Samkhya, Mimamsa, Vedanta and Yoga) that based their credo and curriculum on the study of the ancient Vedas only. Each school interprets differently the macrocosm, symbolised by the universe, and the microcosm of our own mortal bodies. Some have a more academic approach to atoms and molecules; others focus on mind and feelings. But in fact, all these schools of thoughts admit that our own body is a replica of the universe and that there is an aspect to our existence that is more powerful, eternal and infinite than the body itself.

This extraordinary ingredient linked to our lives is our own soul, part of the Cosmic Soul or the absoluteness of God itself. The Vedas call it Atman, the Universal Self, associated to Brahman, the Cosmic Consciousness. Some Vedic schools of philosophy see Atman and Brahman as being totally different entities; others admit the equivalence Atman- Brahman.

Out of all Vedic Darshans, the Yoga philosophy looks deeper into the aspects of life, focusing on both, body and mind, arguing that controlling the mind is the source of a strong body. The theoretical foundation of Yoga school of thought is still based on the Vedic texts, alongside a masterpiece work, created by Sage Maharshi Patanjali. This text, called *"Patanjali Yoga Sutras"*, was produced around 200BC and includes one hundred and ninety six sutras. This work sets the base of the consciousness shift using the superconscious aspect of our controlled minds.

The *"Patanjali Yoga Sutras"* have four chapters that explain the mindset and techniques that enable one to reach the union with the cosmic power called yoga. The first chapter, *"Samadhi Pada"* focuses on concentration, *"Sadhana Pada"* on practices, *"Vibhuti Pada"* on the success achieved if following practices and meditation and the fourth chapter, *"Kaivalya Pada,"* is based on the nature of liberation.

Even if the term Kundalini as we know it now was not used in Patanjali's work, he made an extraordinary statement, which made me think that he was a brilliant scholar of the anatomy of human body.

Patanjali talked about the Naabhi Chakra and its miraculous power. The Naabhi Chakra is in fact the wheel of energy we now know as Manipura, the seat of action and balance. Patanjali argued that Sanyam on this Chakra gives a yogi out of ordinary powers. Sanyam is the term that describes the last three of the eight limbs of yoga, control, integration and restrain, therefore nothing else than the practices of Dharana (concentration), Dhyana (meditation) and Samadhi (union).

Therefore, before neuroscience was able to identify an aspect that makes one achieve Ananda (bliss), Patanjali spotted an area in the human body where the enlightenment may start. The Vagus nerve connects this place. Science agrees now that the Vagus nerve is in charge with swallowing, vocalisation and communication. The Vagus nerve, transmitting impulses from various organs to the brain, communicates information about sexual chemicals and impulses too. This is in fact what we were taught that Tantra does.

Would then be appropriate to say that Kundalini yoga and Tantra are similar? Not at all! Tantra is based on the worship of the feminine aspect of life, the Devi, aiming to achieve the liaison between Shiva and Shakti/ Devi or, if you wish, between Purusha and Prakriti, therefore between matter and consciousness.

Kundalini yoga on the other hand goes much deeper, helping one creating the union with the divine Cosmic Soul through awakening Kundalini. Therefore, if the two have perhaps the same starting point, their final goals are different. However, I admit that Kundalini yoga may have an influence coming from Tantra and Shaktism, the doctrine of energy.

Would then Kundalini yoga and other branches of yoga set

the same targets in reaching the same goals? Well, all yoga schools are focused on achieving the union of the Self with God, the absoluteness. They all do it in different manners based on their own philosophy. Hatha yoga focuses on the physicality of Asanas, Raja yoga on mental control, Bhakti yoga on devotional practices, Shakti yoga on expression of self and Karma yoga on selfless acts… all searching for the dissolution of self and absorption into the cosmic dimension and all awakening Kundalini in a way or another. However the rising of the serpent Shakti is a main goal mostly in Kundalini yoga.

Therefore, without any pride, I would just affirm that Kundalini yoga blends all yoga practices in a product that can be used by each and every person, without the need of extreme physicality or above average intelligence. The way this works is natural and not painful, using Prana or the vital force stored at the base of the spine in order to reprogram the whole brain. This process is possible through awakening Kundalini. This is where the Chakras, Nadis and Granthis are involved in because this practice can happen only if these systems are properly balanced.

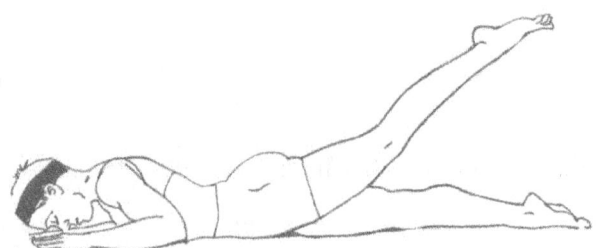

Kundalini yoga aims to work with the Prana Vayu and the Chakras in a natural manner through agitating Kundalini. The practice is simple and, to be perfectly honest, enjoyable. Fast but easy to execute movements, smart breathing techniques and repetition of Mantras form a symbiosis with a final goal in creating the union.

To the skeptical people, I would say that there is neither a mysterious voodoo practice involved in Kundalini awakening, nor an action based on an occult custom. The truth is that if there is an energy stored naturally within us, the process of awakening it should be as genuine too.

I would address to the believers in the existence of Kundalini divine energy in saying that this Shakti is a replica of the astral forces in the universe. I would also argue that Kundalini Shakti is the ether within us. The Sages mentioned ether as the only element existent before creation started manifesting itself. We came from ether and, as we develop spiritually, we are meant to go back to our etheric source.

Whether or not Kundalini is the one and only Source so many enlightened people admit as the forever home for the soul it is up to you to decide. This topic is a matter of choice, perspectives and polarities really. For me though, Kundalini energy is the only true proof that God resides in us. This is the absorption every school of yoga refers to… God in us and us in God!

CHAPTER 7

MANTRA

Mantras are successions of sacred syllables used from the beginning of times as powerful tools in meditation. Mantras are access codes to different channels of our minds; therefore tools to reprogram ourselves. Chanting helps us, yogis, to access higher spiritual connections. To understand the structure of Mantras and how they work, we have to consider sound as vibration.

The Vedas describe sound as an unmanifested form of Brahman itself, the absoluteness, whilst its origin, vibration, as the manifested macrocosm. Sound is the only element able to penetrate Akasha[63], ether, called by science the *"dark energy"*; therefore chanting has the quality of reaching the highest realms.

The Vedic tradition mentions four forms of sounds, all materialised in the shape of speech. Valikhari are the words that make up a language whilst Madhyame refer to the mental speech, mostly connected with how we interpret thoughts through our mental phenomena. Pascyanthi are soundless words, considered to travel at a telepathic level and finally, Para, are the transcendental sounds, similar to the cosmic vibration. Therefore, Mantras are

Para sounds that have the same attributes as the cosmic frequency.

Each Mantra has the same structure really, but a different secret code called Kilaka or Kilah, given by the speed and method of pronunciation.

The pattern of the sacred syllables included in a Mantra is based on three principles: the Pranav, the Bija and the deity it is addressed to. Pranav refers to the origin of the sacred sound in the vibration of *"Om"*. This holly syllable is believed to encompass the power of the whole universe, symbolised by the Trimurti, the Hindu trinity of Brahma, Vishnu and Shiva. Therefore the sacred OM or AUM is called the Pranava Mantra, which form the Udgitha[64] or the song of the universe. Chandogya Upanishad refers to Udgitha as the only succession of sounds that can overcome all obstacles; thus, it acts like an amulet.

The whole universe, our souls included, has its origins in the Pranava Mantra. This Mahamantra (primordial Mantra) is considered *"the monarch of all Mantras"* and the Sage associated with it is Parabrahman, the Supreme Brahman called Nirguna Brahman by Advaita Vedanta school of philosophy. *"Om! This syllable is the whole world"* is the first verse of Mandukya Upanishad.

The Aitareya Brahmana[65], part of Rigveda, links OM, AUM or Omkar to the three stages of creation of the universe. Rigveda Samhita[66] (3.62.10) unites the sacred syllable with Bhur, Bhuvah and Swah, the three realms of existence, forming one of the most famous mantras of all, the Gayatri Mantra. It is believed that this is the origin of the whole knowledge and wisdom contained in the Vedas.

The Bija of each Mantra refers to the seed or the source from which it generated. The seed is a holy sound, vibrating with the

Cosmos' frequency, a sound that has no translatable meaning really. The Omkar itself is a Bija. This seed is the acoustic form of the visual Bindu, which is a little dot placed in the Ajna area in between the eyebrows, reminding of the union with Brahman, from whom creation started.

"Manas (mind) alone are the Bindu. It is the source of creation and preservation" (Kundalini Yoga Upanishad, verse 5). However, Bindu has another meaning in yoga, being the root of the Bindu fluid that contains Amrita[67], God's nectar. This fluid flows in the body and is purified in the Vishuddha.

The syllables, associated with each Chakra, are Bijas too. Therefore when chanted, their vibrations would activate the Chakras. As already mentioned, LAM is linked to Muladhara, VAM to Svadhishthana, RAM to Manipura, YAM to Anahata, HAM to Vishuddha and OM or AUM to both Ajna and Sahasrara.

As yoga has to follow eight limbs, there are six limbs for each Mantra. The first relates to the Rishi who received it in meditation and the next to the deity addressed to; then there is the Bija or the source of a Mantra, as well as the Shakti, or the energy that is involved in chanting it, which gives the power of a certain Mantra. The methods the syllables are grouped have to follow a precise manner, called Chanda.

The last limb of each Mantra is the secret or Kilaka, which is an esoteric lock or perhaps a pillar, hidden in the mantra. To unlock the code, a Mantra has to be chanted repeatedly for many times, usually for one hundred and eight times, according to the Vedic tradition, based on how many Upanishads there are in the Vedas.

However, the number one hundred and eight has a deeper meaning. It refers to the number of units between our bodies and the divine within us. Ayurveda[68], the ancient medical system, considers one hundred and eight Mamma points in our bodies; these being points of the vital force that keeps us alive.

The same sacred number is believed to be related to Anahata that has one hundred and eight energy lines that forms this vortex of energy. However, there is another meaning connected to chanting each Mantra for one hundred and eight times, this number being a Harshad number. What that really means is that it is divisible by the sum of each number that forms it. Translated from Sanskrit, Harshad means *"joy giver"*. Therefore, the chanting tradition considers one hundred and eight Bindus or God multiplied in us.

Kundalini Yoga Upanishad mentions one Mantra involved in awakening the temperamental Kundalini Shakti, consisting of seven syllables, united in the Kechari Mantra, also known as the Melana Mantra. These are: HRIM BHAM SAM PAM PHAM SAM KSHAM. The code of this mantra is still secret and unbreakable. Its effect however is to unlock the Soma Chakra, situated in Sahasrara.

The Soma Chakra[69] is also known as the Amria Chakra or *"the Nectar of the Crescent Moon"* and is symbolised by the shape of the A Ka Tha triangle, considered sacred in the Vedic philosophy. This geometrical shape is also called Karma Kala. Each side of this triangle is formed by a Nadi, symbolising one of the deities in the Trimurti. It is believed that the A Ka Tha triangle is a matrix of the whole creation. At each corner, there is a Bindu, in the shape of the moon, the sun and the eternal fire. All the forty-eight letters of the Sanskrit alphabet start from these three Bindus. The symbol of Kundalini Shakti is in the middle of the sacred triangle.

Because in the Vedic texts Soma is the nectar or the drink of the Devas, the ambrosia that gave them immortality, the Soma Chakra is the emblem of eternity, immortality, the real Sat Shakti, the truth behind Kundalini, the divine energy within us.

There are over twenty thousand Mantras in the Vedas, so plenty to choose from; all following the pattern each mantra should and all having the Kilaka code within.

However, there are a few Mantras that work outside of the magical code; therefore repetition is not to be required. For instance, the Shabar Mantras don't follow the same setup structure. They usually are an amalgam of words from different languages; therefore not composed in Sanskrit. Tradition has it that even if they work on the spot, the Shabar Mantras are weaker and have temporary effects.

KUNDALINI YOGA MANTRAS

Most of Mantras we use in Kundalini yoga are in Gurmukhi, the ancient Sikh language. Gurmukhi means *"from the mouth of the Guru"*, so it is the language of Guru Granth Sahib[70], the main Sikh[71] scripture. However, some of the Kundalini yoga Mantras are in Sanskrit.

ADI Mantra

"Ong Namo Guru Dev Namo"
Translation
"I bow to the Divine Teacher within"

This is the Mantra all Kundalini yogis around the world use to tune in with and it is performed three times at the beginning of a yoga session.

The Adi Mantra uses two powerful representations of God, the Cosmic Absoluteness: *"Ong"* and *"Guru Dev"*. *"Ong"* is the absolute creative energy, whilst *"Guru Dev"* is the universal consciousness.

BIJA Mantra

"Sat Nam"
Translation
"Truth is my identity"

Also called the Seed Mantra, this is the Kundalini yoga greeting. When used in a Kriya, we breathe in when chanting

"Sat" and breathe out at *"Nam"*.

SIRI GAITRI Mantra

"Ra Ma Da Sa Sa Say So Hung"
Traslation
"Sun, moon, earth, infinity: all that is in infinity, I am Thee"

This Mantra is considered one of the most powerful healing chants. *"Ra"* is the sun, *"Ma"* is the moon, *"Da"* is the earth and *"Sa"* is the impersonal infinity, the ether. *"Sa Say"* symbolises the total infinity, *"So"* does the merger with the infinite dimension and *"Hung"* is the vibration of infinity.

ANTAR NAAD Mantra

"Sa Re Sa Sa"
Translation
"The infinite is here and everywhere".

It is said that this Mantra removes any negativity.

ADI SHAKTI Mantra

*"Ek Ong Kar, Sat Nam
Siri Wahe Guru"*
Translation
*"There is only one Creator whose name is Truth.
Great is the ecstasy of the Supreme Wisdom"*

The Adi Shakti Mantra is one of the main Mantras involved in awakening Kundalini Shakti.

"Ek" is the essence of all, *"Ong"* is the manifested vibration of God, *"Kar"* is the creation, *"Sat"* is the vibration of truth, *"Nam"* is the name or identity, *"Siri"* is the greatness of God, *"Wha"* is

ecstasy and *"Guru"* is God itself, who takes us from darkness to light.

MANGALA CHARAN Mantra

"Aad Guray Nameh
Jugad Guray Nameh
Sat Guray Nameh
Siri Guru Dayvay Nameh"
Translation
"I bow to the Primal Wisdom,
I bow to the Universal Wisdom,
I bow to the True Wisdom,
I bow to the Unseen Wisdom"

This Mantra is also called the *"White Light Mantra of the Sukhmani Sahib"*, being one of the main protection chants.

GURU GAITRI Mantra

"Gobinday, Mukanday, Udharay, Aparay
Hariang, Kariang, Nirnamay, Akamay"
Translation
"Sustainer, Liberator, Enlightener, Infinite,
Destroyer, Creator, Nameless, Desireless"

It is believed that the Guru Gaitri Mantra helps one removing all karmic blockages.

KIRTAN Mantra

"Sa Ta Na Ma"

This Mantra contains the five primordial sounds of the Universe: S, T, N, M and A. *"Sa"* stands for beginning of the Universe, *"Ta"* for existence, *"Na"* for transformation and *"Ma"* for rebirth.

HEART OPENING Mantra

"Ong So Hung"
Translation
"Creator, I am Thou"

This Mantra opens Anahata and is usually chanted by Kundalini yogis to honor their connection with God. *"Ong"* is God's consciousness and *"So Hung"* means *"I am that"*.

GURU RAM DAS Mantra

"Guru Guru Wahe Guru
Guru Ram Das Guru"

This Mantra calls upon Ram Das in praise for protective guidance and light. Guru Ram Das was the founder of Ramdaspur, the holly city of Amritsar. This Mantra opens all seven Chakras.

HARI Mantra

"Hari Nam, Sat Nam

Hari Nam, Hari"

This Mantra helps one connecting to the consciousness of God. *"Hari"* is the Supreme Absolute in the universe. It also aligns the flow of life and our own identity.

SPIRIT Mantra

"Hume Hum
Brahm Hum"
Translation
"We are We

We are God"

This Mantra is considered the Mantra of creative expression that cleans the spirit.

AQUARIAN AGE MANTRAS

After living for far too long in the Piscean Age, we entered into the Aquarian Age. In the mental Piscean age, everything was about learning more, doing more, having more and wanting more. Competition ruled every day of our lives and showing off was the only way of living. We needed teachers, masters, gurus to get closer to God because we felt we were never enough.

Astrologers calculated the starting point of the Aquarian Age as being on the eleventh November 2011 (11.11.11). They considered the move of the star Regulus from the Piscean to the Aquarian constellation and affirmed that we will stay in this very special age for a long period of time.

Stepping into the Aquarian Age was a relief. We now understand that we are our own teachers, masters or gurus and we don't have to follow anybody who promises enlightenment and liberation. Therefore, we embraced the motto *"Be to be"*. We learnt enough to know how to connect to the Supreme Reality and we don't need a mediator between God and us anymore. Therefore, we have new Mantras celebrating the liberating age of the Aquarius, each of them helping us create a bridge from us to God.

WAAH YANTE Mantra

"Waah Yanthi, Kar Yanthi
Jag Dut Patee
Aadak Ik Waaha
Brahmadeh Tresha Guru
It Wahe Guru"

Translation
"Great Macroself, Creative Self
All that is creative through time,
All that is the Great One.
Three aspects of God:
Brahma, Vishnu, Mahesh
That is Wahe Guru"

SAT SIRI Mantra

"Sat Siri, Siri Akal
Siri Akal, Maha Akal
Maha Ahal, Sat Nam
Akal Murat, Waheguru"
Translation
"Great Truth, Great Undying,
Great Undying, Great Deathless
Great Deathless, Truth is God's name
Deathless Image of God"

AAD SACH Mantra

"Aad Sach
Jugad Sach
Haibhee Sach
Nanak Hosee Bhee Sach"
Translation
"True in the beginning
True through all the ages
True even now
Nanak says True shall ever be"

AQUARIAN SADHANA Mantra

"Har, Har, Nam Nidham Hai
Hai Guramukh Paeia Jae"
Translation
"The name of God Har
is the greatest treasure.
Gurmukhs obtain it"

Gurmucks refers to everybody who is attuned to God.

WAHE GURU Mantra

"Wahe Guru
Wahe Jio"
Translation
"God is great!"

Wahe Guru is called the *"Mantra of ecstasy"*.

MUL Mantra

"Ek Ong Kar, Sat Nam
Karta Purkh, Nirbho, Nirvair
Akal Murat Ajoonee
Saibung Gur Prasad
Aad Sach
Jugad Sach
Hai Bhee Sach
Nanak Hosee Bhee Sach"
Translation
"One true Creator and Creation
Doer of everything, fearless, revengeless
Undying, Unborn

KUNDALINI, THE DIVINE WITHIN

Self-Existent is Guru's grace
True in the beginning
True through all times
True even now
Nanak says True shall ever be"

VEDIC MANTRAS

There are many Vedic Mantras I like to chant. I found them as powerful reminders of my union with God.

SURYA GAYATRI Mantra (in Rigveda)

"Om Bhur Bhuvah
Tat Savitur Varenyan
Bhargo Devasya Dhimahi
Dhiyo Yo Nah Pga Codayat"
Translation
"Om, earth, sky and heaven
May we place within ourselves
The radiance of the Divine Surya
Who shall awaken our insight"

PAVAMANA Mantra (In Brihadaranyaka Upanishad)

"Asato Ma Sad Gamaya
Tamaso Ma Jyotin Gamaya
Mrtyor Ma Amritam Gamaya"
Translation
"Lead us from unreal to real
Lead us from darkness to light
Lead us from death to immortality"

ISHA Mantra (In Isha Upanishad)

"Purnam Adah Purnam Idam
Purnam Purnam Udachiate

Purnasya Purnam
Adaya Purnam Evavashishyat"
Translation
"That is whole, that is whole
The whole arises from the whole
Having taken the whole from the whole
Only the whole remains"

SOHAM Mantra (in Isha Upanishad)

"Soham"
Translation
"I am that"

FIVE ELEMENTS Mantra (in Krishna Yajurveda)

"Om Namah Shivaya"

This Mantra from Krishna Yajurveda, includes the five elemental powers: *"Na"* for earth, *"Ma"* for water, *"Si"* for fire, *"Va"* for pranic air and *"Ya"* for ether.

SIX SYLABLE Mantra (in Mantrayana Sutra)

"Om Mani Padme Hum"
Translation
"Praise the jewel in the lotus"

BLESSING Mantra

"Lokhah Samastah Sukhino Bhabantu"
Translation
"May all the beings everywhere be happy"

CHAPTER 8

MUDRA

Many people believe that Mudras are gesture performed with the hands only; therefore called Hasta Mudras. The truth is that there are feet Mudras as well as symbolic gestures performed with the head (Mana Mudras), postural (Kaya Mudras) and even Mudras executed with the tongue (Kechari Mudra), all having the same purpose of sealing energy. Translated from Sanskrit, a Mudra means exactly that: a seal. Even the three yogic Bandhas are in fact variations of Mudras. Therefore Mudras are locks of energy, mostly performed in yoga, but in dance too.

In yoga, these symbolical gestures are usually executed simultaneously with special Pranayama techniques in order to activate special parts in the body. In fact, there are minor Chakras in the palms that are activated whilst fingers Mudras are completed. There are also many nerve endings and three main nerves in the fingers, Radial, Ulnar and Median, and activating them may trigger a series of reflexes.

Each finger of a hand is associated with one of the five main elements in the universe, called Pancha Boota[72], the source of the universal or cosmic creation. Therefore, the index finger is linked to Vayu (air), the middle finger to Akasha (ether), the ring finger to Prithvi (earth), the small finger to Apas (water) and the thumb to Agni (fire). By connecting together two or more fingers, therefore the elements associated to them, one is able to balance the energies and create a harmonious life force flow in the body.

Each element linked in the microcosm represented by a finger is also associated to an organ of sense. Vayu and the index finger is related to the skin, Akasha and the middle finger to the ears, Prithvi and the ring finger to the nose, Apas and the small finger to the tongue and Agni and the thumb to the eyes.

The fingers of our hands are connected with the energy of the planets in the universal macrocosm. Therefore, the index finger is called the Jupiter finger, the middle one is the Saturn finger, the ring finger is linked to Venus, the small finger to Mercury and the thumb to Mars.

Even if Brahmins[73], the high caste of priests, used Mudras, I personally haven't found a Vedic text dedicated to these seals of energy, other than perhaps the Bandhas and the Kechari Mudra. However, the Vedic rituals involved Mudras as well as chanting the Vedas.

Tradition has it that some Mudras are able to cleanse part of the karma; but let's be honest here. A Mudra cannot heal a body part and cannot wipe the past either. What it can do though is to stimulate parts of the brain, help concentrating, get in tune in meditation and clean the mind of unwanted thoughts. I believe that Mudras can also attract positive energies. Even Carl Jung agreed: *"Often the hands will solve a mystery the intellect has struggled with in vain"*.

Mudras are powerful tools used by yoga movement from

ancient times and, together with breathing, Asanas and Mantras, create an environment for spiritual awakening.

MAIN MUDRAS IN KUNDALINI YOGA

ANJALI Mudra

Also called the *"Prayer Mudra"*, Anjali is performed by pressing the palms together at the chest level, with the thumbs pressed firmly in the sternum.

Anjali means *"to offer"* or *"to salute"*. This Mudra opens Anahata. In the yogic community, it is known as the *"Seal of salutation"*.

GYAN Mudra

This Mudra is the *"Seal of knowledge"*. It is performed by touching the tip of the thumb with the tip of the index finger.

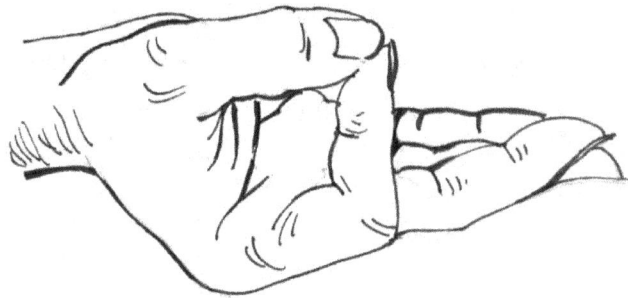

SHUNI Mudra

It is known as the *"Seal of patience"*. It is performed by touching the tip of the thumb with the tip of the middle finger.

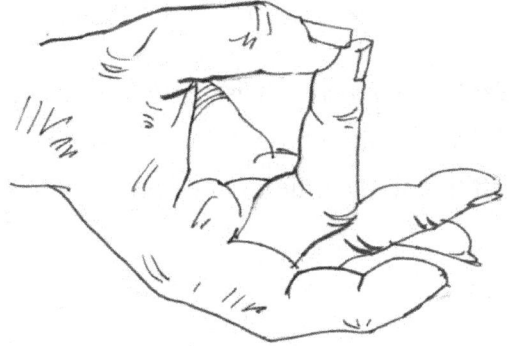

SURYA Mudra

Also called Ravi Mudra, this is the *"Seal of life"*. It is performed by touching the tip of the thumb with the tip of the ring finger.

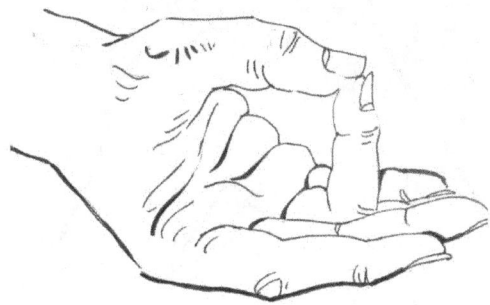

BUDDHI Mudra

This is the *"Seal of mental clarity"*. It is performed by touching the tip of the thumb with the tip of the small finger.

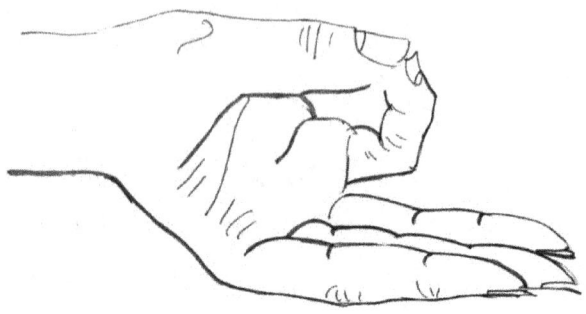

VENUS lock

This is the *"Seal of balance"*. It is performed by interlocking the fingers of both hands with the right thumb above the left thumb for men and the left thumb over the right thumb for women.

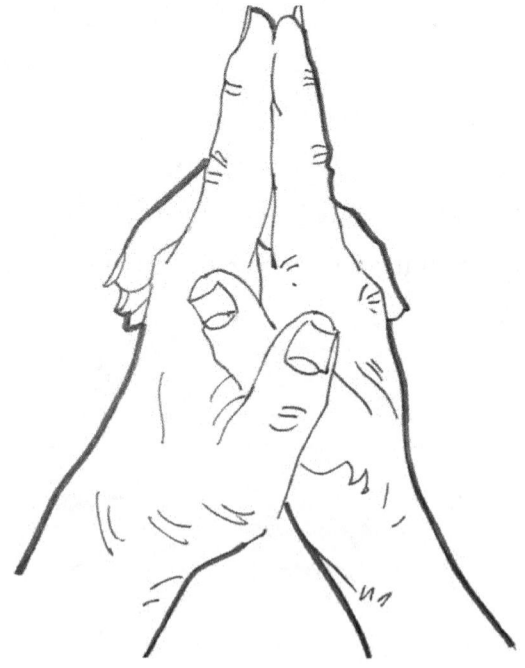

BUDDHA Mudra

This is the *"Seal of concentration"*. It is performed by resting the right hand on top of the left hand for men and the left hand on top of the right hand for women, whilst thumbs are touching.

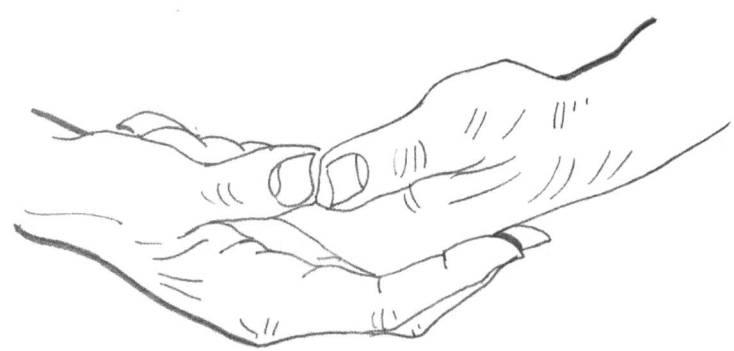

BANDHAS

MULA BHANDHA

Performed in three steps:
1. Sit in Sukhasana (easy pose) and contract the muscles of the rectum
2. Contract the muscles of the perineum
3. Hold your breath and draw the lower abdomen back towards your spine.

UDDIYANA BHANDHA

Sit in Sushasana (easy pose). Exhale. Suck in your solar plexus and lift your diaphragm. This would create a cavity in the stomach area.

JALANDHARA BHANDHA

Performed in three steps:
1. Sit in Sukhasana (easy pose) with the palms facing upwards

on your knees. Inhale deeply.
2. Drop your chin down and lift the sternum towards the chin. Your shoulders should be relaxed.
3. Hold and then lift your chin and release the breath

CHAPTER 9

MEDITATION

The source of the union yoga talks about is meditation and the root cause of spiritual Kundalini awakening starts with it. The world used in Sanskrit for this practice is Dhyana, with the origin in *"dhi"*, which means *"imaginary vision"*. This concept appears as a path to Samadhi in most books of the Vedas and explained in the Brahma Sutras, main text for Vedanta philosophy. However, it is in the *"Yoga Sutras of Patajali"* (1.20) where the main five keys to enlightenment are debated.

Shaddha or unconditional faith is the first step, followed by Virrya or will power and Smriti or mindfulness. In order to achieve Samadhi, the absorption in the cosmic realms, one would also need Prajna or wisdom, Purvakah or prerequisite and Itaresam or other people.

The Yoga Sutras don't talk about blind faith in anything and everything whatsoever. The faith mentioned in the texts is the belief that we are only a small part of the universe; also that there should be something grander that makes it harmonious. But in most cases, this is not enough. One would need to be focused and determined to reach the union with God, therefore mindful of the challenge and wise enough to absorb knowledge from the sources that count, trustful people and texts.

Samadhi is the stillness of mind, a state that can be achieved only in meditation, a level where the theta brain waves are fully active.

In every meditation process, there are usually two phases involved. The first is Dharana, which is focusing on the object of contemplation, followed by Dhyana itself or full meditative state. Kundalini yoga follows the same two steps. In the first stage of most meditation Kriyas, the attention is brought to a fixed point in the body, usually in between the eyebrows, where Ajna is situated.

A spiritual being has to absorb life from a spiritual perspective. There is no doubt about that. Therefore, how can this be achieved if the mind is involved in constant material thoughts based on the physicality of this world? Well, the answer is the way the mind can be directed to create the mental activity necessary for the spiritual foundation.

Vedanta philosophy accepts four abilities that work together in creating mental activity. They are Manas or the mind, Buddhi, the intelligence, Ahamkara, the self or the ego, and Citta or the dimension of storing information.

Manas with the organ senses are the observers of the reality and the organisers of our daily lives. Buddhi is in charge with the knowledge coming from either external or internal sources. Ahamkara gives our identity, making the separation between us and others, whilst Citta is in control of our memories. We think because of Manas, learn because of Buddhi, identify ourselves because of Ahamkara and recall experiences because of Chitta.

Two of these parts play essential roles in meditation: the loud

Manas and the quiet Buddhi.

The whole purpose of contemplation is quieting down the Manas and putting Buddhi in charge. Manas would easily give in though if Ahamkara would not be that strong willed. So the only solution really is to strengthen Buddhi. However, this would happen not necessarily through the process of meditation itself. It has to be initiated prior through the life we live and the choices we make. Therefore the question arising is if we are focused in our mundane activities on the supreme truth or on the fakeness provided by our modern lives.

According to the Tantric tradition, Buddhi is the faculty that allows acknowledging Atman. Buddhi is in charge with discriminating between what helps us and what is useless for our development. We comprehend, act and analyse because of it, so it makes sense working on the intelligent faculty of our minds in order to take control of our lives. The same Tantric tradition points out that as less developed the Buddhi as more attached one is to desires for sense objects. Thus, the solution stays in detaching from the material reality through meditation and accumulating constant knowledge of things that matter.

We would be able to detach ourselves from the noisy nonsense and meditate only if we live a life based on Sat (truth). For the restless, busy, here and there individual, meditation is not possible. *"The yogi should keep the Manas in the midst of Shakti and the Shakti in the midst of Manas"* (Kundalini Yoga Upanishad).

Sat is one of the qualities of Atma, the soul, alongside Cit or consciousness and Ananda, the state of true happiness, the eternal bliss. Atma or Atman is our real identity, the inner consciousness, so we have to live according to it.

Kundalini yoga acknowledges the truth and strengthens Buddhi through daily Sadhana, the spiritual practice or exercise, in which repetitions of Mantras allow the awakening process to begin. Buddhi comes from the Sanskrit root *"budh"* that means *"to be awake"*, a quality of our own identity Kundalini yoga uses. Therefore it goes beyond the Doctrine of the Three Bodies, arguing that our identity is based on ten bodies, one physical, three mental and six energetic bodies.

The three mental bodies are layers of the negative mind, the positive mind and the neutral mind. If the negative mind identifies dangers, whilst the positive mind trusts that we are exactly where we should be, the neutral aspect of our mind is in charge with the meditative state. Therefore, being neutral, whilst accessing situations is the work we would need to focus on prior trying to quiet the mind.

Awareness and meditation bring us together with our energetic layers, our soul that is immortal and eternal, our archline or halo, our aura, pranic body, subtle body and ultimately the radiant body.

CHAPTER 10

KUNDALINI YOGA

Also known as the *"Yoga of Awareness"*, Kundalini yoga has its origins in the ancient times, being first mentioned in the Upanishads. Because it was considered a sacred style of yoga, having its roots in the ancient Laya yoga, Kundalini yoga was kept secret for thousands of years; being passed on only from a guru or a master to a chosen disciple.

Kundalini yoga never spread outside of the secret yoga society until the late 1960's when a Sikh, who called himself Yogi Bhajan[74], started teaching it in the American continent and declared it *"the yoga of the householder"*. Thus, with the layers of mysteries peeled one after another, from secret and hidden, Kundalini yoga became accessible to everybody.

Since then, the Kundalini yoga community grew immensely as millions of people wanted to experience the ancient sacred yoga of uncoiling the snake called Kundalini and the promised spiritual enlightenment. Studios appeared all around the world like mushrooms after rain and the Kundalini Kula of yogis wearing white only got bigger with each day. Alongside average people, celebrities joined the movement and brought Kundalini yoga in the limelight. And there is no wonder why!

If you have ever attended a Kundalini yoga class, you would know what I am talking about. If you didn't, there is still time! The whole atmosphere oozes joy, happiness and love. We are known as the yogis who can sing, exactly as the pre-Vedic Vratyas[72] tribes did. They developed a cult for Pranayama only to be able to master singing. We do the same to worship the God within us.

And then there are the Kundalini yoga festivals, where thousands of people from all around the world come together in the name of oneness and love for the whole creation. So there is just fair that in just a few years since some of its secrets were revealed, Kundalini yoga became a trend for the rich and a must for the middle class.

Kundalini yoga philosophy is based on the concept that each human is a vessel for reaching the Brahmanic consciousness; also that the union with the Cosmic Consciousness can be achieved if the holy Kundalini energy is awakened. Therefore, Kundalini yoga is beyond fitness, stretching and flexibility; it is a philosophy and a science.

Kundalini yoga bases its practice on Kriyas, which are sequences of Pranayama (breathing), Asanas (postures), Bandhas (body locks), Mantras, Mudras and special meditations. Some say that there are over two thousand Kriyas and over five thousand meditations. To be perfectly honest, I believe that there are many more, because each teacher usually designs theirs. However, Kundalini Yoga Upanishad mentions only one that is related to awakening Kundalini Shakti.

And then there is the Kundalini yoga tradition, a heritage that passed from one generation to another... Some people wonder why

Kundalini yogis wear white only. Well, there are a few explanations. Firstly, it is believed that colours play a significant influence on one's aura. It is also said that white extends one's auric field; therefore expanding positivity. White is the colour of purity and innocence and white helps one focus to introspection.

All Kundalini yogis cover their heads with a white turban or scarf. There are reasons behind this tradition too. It is said that a tight head covering creates cranial adjustment, which may help with the focus on Ajna, the Third Eye Chakra. A head covering also improves the flow of energy from the head towards the lower extremities.

Kundalini yoga is the real deal... at least for me. Starting with the whole atmosphere of joy and happiness, as an effect of yoga and music, and finishing with the amazing benefits of this style of yoga, flexibility, wellbeing, peace, harmony and the promise of Kundalini awakening...

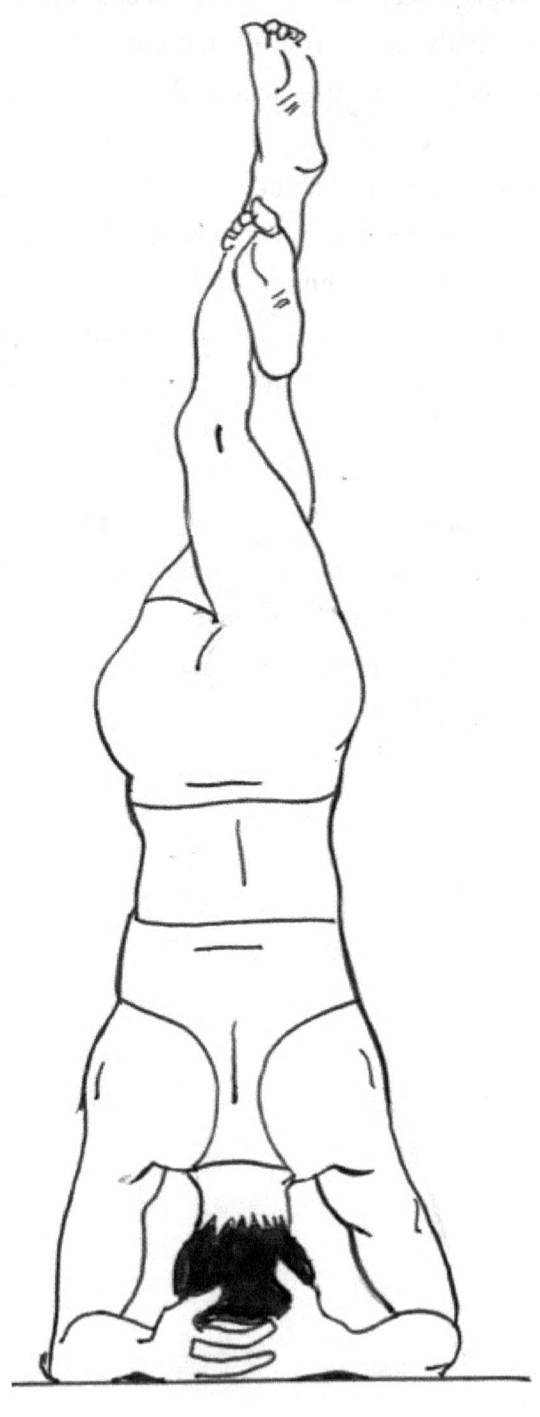

KUNDALUNI YOGA PRANAYAMA

Breathing is not under our conscious control. We all inhale and exhale air, but do we breathe in and out correctly? Well, the answer is no. For organs, muscles and tissues to be properly oxygenated, the capacity of the air inhaled and exhaled should have the same value and this is not always the case.

In Kundalini yoga, there are breathing techniques used in other branches of yoga and Pranayama performed only in Kundalini yoga.

BREATH OF FIRE
(Agni Prasana)

This breathing technique is specific to Kundalini yoga only.

The Breath of Fire is a rapid, rhythmic and continuous breathing through the nose only with inhaling and the exhaling having the same length. The focus however is on a powerful exhaling. With every breathe in, the abdominal muscles relax and with every breathe out, the diaphragm lifts upward whilst the abdominal muscles are pulled in quickly.

The main benefit of this Pranayama is detoxifying the blood and the mucous linings.

CANNON BREATING

This is the Breath of Fire breathing, done through the mouth only. It adjusts digestion.

ALTERNATE NOSTRIL BREATHING

(Nadi Shodana)

Whilst sitting comfortably, start with exhaling on the left nostril whilst your thumb covers your right nostril. Release your nostril and inhale on your right nostril whilst your thumb is placed on the left nostril. Exhale deeply on your right nostril.

Next, cover your right nostril and inhale deeply on your left nostril; then exhale on the same nostril.

You may want to repeat the process for two or three more times.

Nadi Shodana regulates the nervous system and balances Ida and Pingala.

LION BREATHING

This is an excellent Pranayama for activating Vishuddha. To perform it, extend the tongue towards your chin; then breathe in and out over the root of the tongue.

SITALI

This Pranayama has a profound cooling effect. It is excellent for cooling when affected by an over warming Pingala Nadi. Breathing in is through a curled in a *"U"* shape tongue and breathing out through the nose.

VATSKAR

This Pranayama is based on sipping air in the lungs only. Therefore, inhaling is done by sipping in eight times, whilst exhaling slowly through the nose in one long exhale.

SITKARI

This Pranayama has a cleansing effect. It is performed by breathing in through the teeth and breathing out through the nose.

WHISLE BREATHING

This Pranayama works on the thyroid and parathyroid glands. To perform it, inhale through a puckered mouth by making a whistle noise; then exhale through the nose.

SEGMENTED BREATING

In this Pranayama, the inhalation and exhalation are divided in intervals. In Kundalini yoga, there are five setup intervals we use:
- for an energising effect: one part inhale, four parts exhale
- for clarity: equal four parts inhale and exhale
- for focus: eight parts inhale and four parts exhale
- for relaxing: four parts inhale and eight parts exhale
- for calming: equal eight parts inhale and exhale

KUNDALINI YOGA ASANAS

SUKHASANA

(Easy pose)

Also called the easy pose, Sukhasana is a very relaxing pose. Sit cross-legged with the spine straight and a widened and expanded rib cage.

PADMASANA

(Lotus pose)

This asana needs flexibility; therefore time to master it. As you are sitting with your legs straight in front of you, bend your right leg and bring it to the crease of your left hip.

The sole of your right foot faces upwards. Bend your left knee and cross your left ankle over the top of your right shin so the sole of your left foot faces upwards too.

BHUJANGASANA
(Cobra pose)

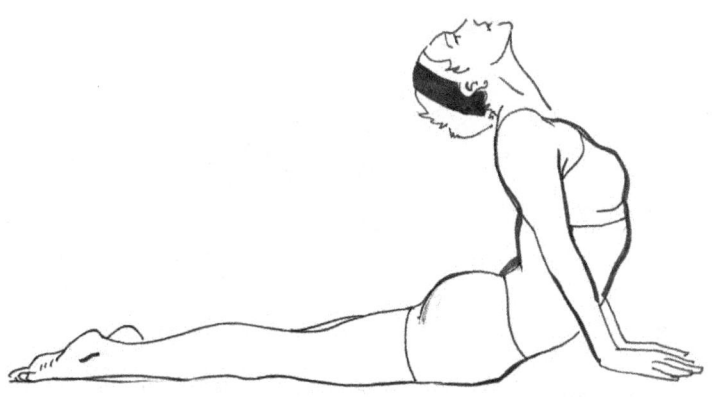

Lie on your tummy, facing the floor with your hands under the shoulders and flat on the floor. Push up, lifting the heart and keeping the pelvis on the floor.

NAVASANA

(Boat pose)

As you are sitting with the legs straightforward, bend slowly backwards and bring your legs up. Your torso and legs should form a *"V"* shape. Keep your knees bent if you feel discomfort.

USTRASANA

(Camel pose)

Kneel with your thighs perpendicular to the floor. As you are drawing your hands up the sides of your body, bring your hips slowly forward so they stay over your knees. Let your head go back, opening your throat. You may need time and practice to be able to reach your heels.

GURU PRANAM
(Child pose)

Sit on the heels and bring your torso over your thighs. Place your forehead on the floor and extend the hands at the back.

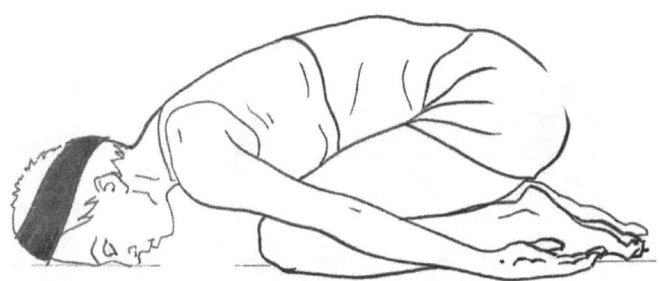

VAJRASANA

(Rock pose)

Sit on your heels with your back straight.

DHANURASANA

(Bow pose)

Lie on your belly. As you exhale, bend your knees and bring

your feet as close as possible to buttocks. Reach and hold your ankles. Inhale and lift your thighs away from the floor.

MARJARYASANA & BITILASANA
(Cat & Cow pose)

Cat: Start with palms and knees on the floor and elbows and shoulders in perfect line. Inhale and whilst exhaling, round your spine upwards and release your head towards the floor.

Cow: Start with palms and knees on the floor and elbows and shoulders in perfect line. Inhale and whilst exhaling, sink your belly towards the floor and lift your head to look straightforward.

AKARNA DHANURASANA
(Archer pose)

Stand up with your feet together; then rotate your right foot around 45 degrees and step back. Bend your left knee, making sure it doesn't go past your left foot. Rotate your upper body to the left and bend your right elbow. Bring your right fist toward your right armpit. Thumbs face upwards. Look forward.

SARVANGASANA
(Shoulder stand)

Lie on the floor with your hands beside the body. Exhale and gently raise your legs, keeping your knees straight. Balance the body weight on your palms. Lift your arms towards the waist with the fingers extended to the back of your hips and the thumbs towards the navel.

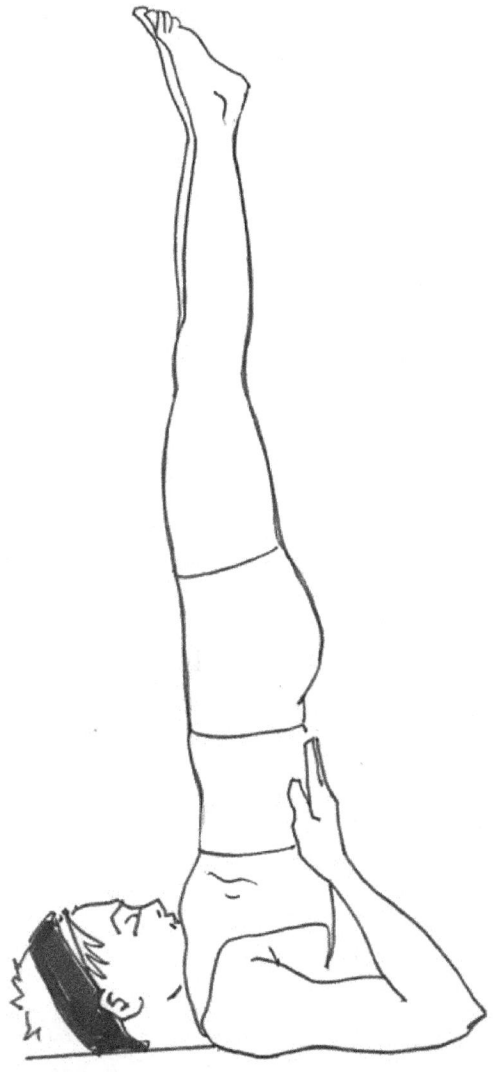

SETU BANDHA SARVAGASANA
(Bridge pose)

Lie on the floor with the knees bent and the feet firm on the floor. Exhale as you lift your hips towards the ceiling. Keep your thighs and feet parallel.

Extend your arm and reach towards the ankles.

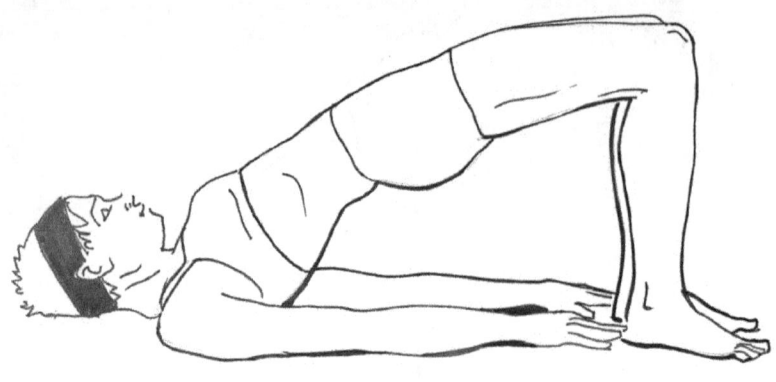

BAKASANA
(Crawl pose)

This is an advanced pose with a positive effect on Sahasrara. Move very gently to Bakasana whilst lifting slowly one foot of the ground and leaning one knee into your triceps. Very slowly shift your weight forward and lift the other foot.

HALASANA
(Plow pose)

Lie on your back with the arms beside you. Inhale and raise your legs at 90 degrees. Support your back with your hands. Nicely sweep your legs at 180 degrees over your head. Make sure your back is perpendicular to the floor.

PURVOTTANASANA
(Upward Plank pose)

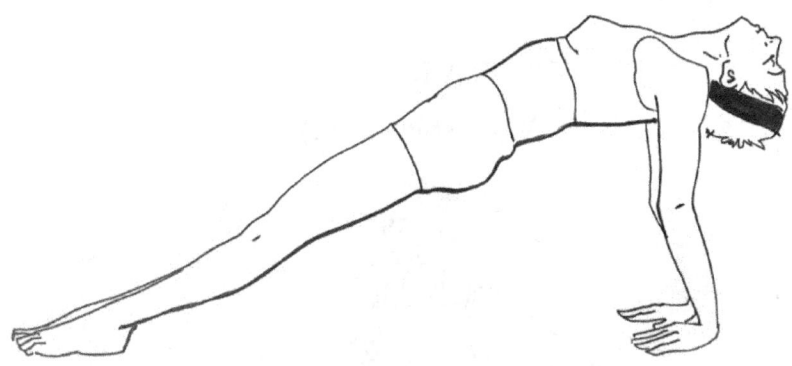

Lie on your back. Exhale whilst you bring your hips up into a reverse tabletop position. Your feet should be firmly pushing down.

Support the lift of the chest by pressing your shoulder blades against your back torso. Slowly drop your head down.

ADHO MUKHA SAVASANA
(Kundalini Triangle)

Start on your palms and knees. Exhale and lift your knees up, stretching out your arms. Slowly straighten your knees and fully extend your arms.

UPVISHTA KONASANA
(Wide splits pose)

This is a pose you may need to practice for long time. You may start in half splits and work your way towards it. In Kundalini yoga it is usually used with alternate bends to one of the legs.

SUPTA VIRASANA
(Reclining Hero pose)

Star in Rock pose with the hands besides on the floor. Bring your hands back towards your buttock and bend backwards. To come on your forearms, bend your elbows.

CHAPTER 11

KUNDALINI YOGA KRIYAS

For an outsider, a Kundalini yoga class may seem simple. Well, I assure you that it is not. The movements are fast, the meditation is deep and the Breath of Fire is not for everybody. Therefore, I would suggest starting slow. There is no need to rush! Remember that yoga is all about passion, dedication and commitment.

But because Kundalini yoga is the yoga of the householder, I included some Kriyas that helped me during the years and I would advise you all, lovers of this style of yoga, to take one step at the time and build up stamina and flexibility of your body and mind. The last thing you need is an injury. Therefore, always remember that big achievements take time.

Be even more cautious if you have an injury that caused you trouble lately. Ask your doctor or your trainer, if you have one, what you can and cannot do. And remember to enjoy every moment of your path to enlightenment with yoga.

KIRTAN MEDITATION

Tune in with Adi Mantra
Asana: Sukhasana or Padmasana
Mantra: Sa Ta Na Ma

Mudras:
- Gyan Mudra when chanting SA
- Shuni Mudra when chanting TA
- Surya Mudra when chanting NA
- Bhudhi Mudra when chanting MA

Focus: with the eyes closed, focus on Ajna
Time: 15 to 30 minutes

Sit in Sukhasana or Padmasana with the back perfectly straight.

For the first 5 minutes, chant with normal voice; then for another 5 whisper the Mantra. The last 5 minutes, chant silently in your own head. Repeat the cycle.

To end: Bring your arms above the head as you would swipe your aura. Inhale as you raise your arms and exhale whilst you bring them down.

SUSHMUNA MANTRA MEDITATION
(MEDITATION FOR HEALING)

Tune in with Adi Mantra

Asana: Sukhasana or Padmasana

Mantra: Ra Ma Da Sa Sa Say So Hung

Mudra: Bend down your elbows by the sides and against the ribs with the palms facing upwards and parallel with the floor

Focus: With the eyes closed, focus on the person you want to bring healing to

Time: 11 to 31 minutes

SAT KRIYA
(AQUARIAN AGE KRIYA)

Tune in with Adi Mantra
Asana: Sukhasana or Rock pose
Mantra: Sat Nam
Mudra: Anjali Mudra
Focus: with the eyes closed, focus on Ajna
Time: 3 to 31 minutes

Chant SAT as you pull the navel in towards the spine. Chant NAM as you relax the stomach.

To end: Inhale and contract the muscles in your torso. Exhale and hold the breath up to 20 seconds. Inhale and relax.

MEDITATION FOR DEEP SLEEP

Tune in with Adi Mantra
Asana: Sukhasana
Mantra: Sa Ta Na Ma Wahe Guru
Mudra: Bear Mudra
Time: 11 to 31 minutes
Pranayama: Inhale in 4 sniffs whilst mentally repeat the first part of the Mantra: Sa Ta Na Ma. Exhale in 2 strokes whilst mentally repeat the second part: Wahe Guru.
Benefits: This Kriya relaxes the nervous system and helps having a good sleep. Practice it as a bedtime meditation.

EGO ERADICATOR
(MAGNETIC FIELD)

Tune in with Adi Mantra

Asana: Sukhasana or Padmasana

Mudra: Fingers fond onto the mounds and thumbs are up. Palms are stretched wide, pulling the knuckles back.

Pranayama: Breath of Fire

Bandha: Jalandhara Bandha

Focus: to Sahasrara

Time: 3 minutes

Sit in Sukhasana or Rock pose and raise your arms up to 60 degrees, keeping your shoulders down and your elbows straight. Apply Jalandhara Bandha (neck lock).

To end: Inhale whilst bringing your arm overhead with the thumbs touching. Exhale whilst opening the fingers and bringing the arms down.

ARCHER KRIYA
(FOR MANIPURA)

Tune in with Adi Mantra

Asana: Archer pose (also called the Hero pose)

Mudra: Curl the fingers into the palms with thumbs pulled back

Pranayama: Breath of Fire

Focus: Gaze at the thumb in front of you

Time: 3 minutes on each side

Bring the right foot forward (left foot is a 45 degrees). Right knee is bent; left knee is straight. Imagine yourself pulling back a bow and arrow.

RELEASE STRESS KRIYA
(BEGINNING OF THE DAY MEDITATION)

Tune in with Adi Mantra
Asana: Sukhasana or Padmasana
Mudra: Gyan Mudra
Pranayama: Inhale through the nose in 8 equal parts; exhale deeply in 1 part
Focus: on the breath
Time: 3 to 11 minutes
To end: Inhale deeply and hold the breath for up to 20 seconds whilst rolling your shoulders very slowly; exhale powerfully. Inhale deeply and hold the breath for up to 20 seconds whilst rolling your shoulders fast; exhale powerfully and relax for 1 minute.

LAYA YOGA MEDITATION

Asana: Sukhasana or Padmasana
Mantra: Ek Ong Kar
    Sa Ta Na Ma
    Siri Wahe Guru
Mudra: Anjali Mudra above your head
Bandha: Apply Uddiyana Bandha whilst chanting Ek Ong Kar
Focus: on the flow of spinal energy up to Sahasrara
Time: Start with 5 minutes and build up in time to 11 to 31 minutes
Benefits: This meditation awakens awareness

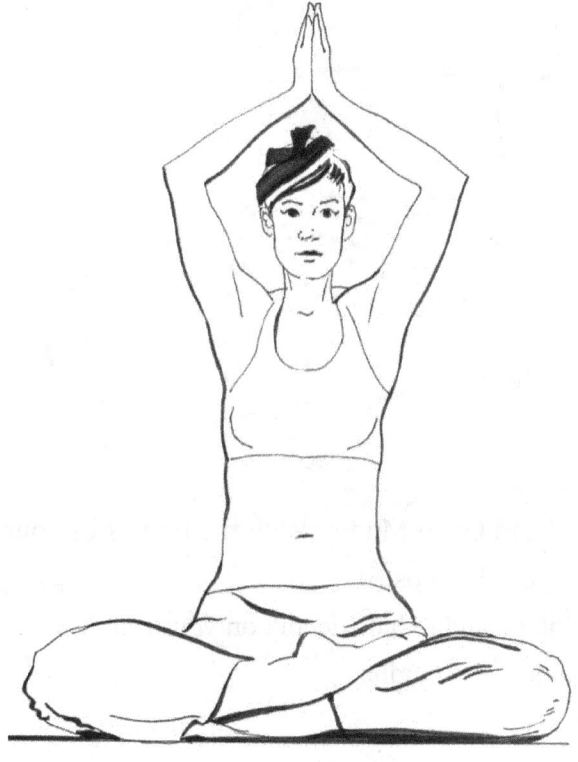

BEGINNER KRIYA

Tune in with Adi Mantra
PINGALA BALANCE

Asana: Sukhasana
Mudra: Right hand Gyan Mudra. With the fingers of your left hand cover your left nostril
Pranayama: Inhale and exhale deeply on your right nostril
Bandha: engage Mula Bandha
Focus: on Ajna
Time: 1 minute

IDA BALANCE

Asana: Sukhasana
Mudra: Left hand on your knee. With the fingers of your right hand cover your right nostril
Pranayama: Inhale and exhale deeply on your left nostril
Bandha: engage Mula Bandha
Focus: on Ajna
Time: 1 minute

PINGALA BALANCE

Asana: Sukhasana
Mudra: Gyan Mudra
Pranayama: Breath in and out through your nose, making sure that inhaling and exhaling have the same length
Focus: on Ajna
Time: 2 minutes

SPINAL TWIST

Asana: Sit in Sukhasana with hands on your shoulders.
Time: 2 minutes

BEND FORWARD

Asana: Sit with the legs straight in front. Hold your toes with your fingers and start bending forward.
Pranayama: Inhale as you bend forward and exhale as you are coming back.

Time: 2 minutes

CAT COW

Asana: Cat Cow
Pranayama: Inhale as you are going to Cow pose and exhale as you are going to Cat pose.
Time: 2 minutes

MEDITATION

Asana: Sukhasana

Mudra: Venus lock above your head
Mantra: Sat Nam
Pranayama: Inhale deeply and chant long Sat and short Nam.
Time: 3 to 5 minutes

ENERGISING KRIYA

Tune in with Adi Mantra

Life nerve stretch: Sit with your left leg stretched out in front of you and right foot against the inner thigh. Hold for 1 minute your left foot with both hands. Then hold for 1 minute the right foot with both hands.

Basic spine flex: Sit in Sukhasana holding your knees.

Inhale as you lift the chest high. Exhale whilst rounding

your lower back. Keep the chin parallel to the floor. Repeat for 3 minutes

Cat- Cow: Position yourself on hands and knees. Fingers are pointing forward. Inhale whilst lowing your spine down and stretching the head and neck back (Cow pose). Exhale whilst arching your spine up and stretching your neck and bring your chin to the chest (Cat pose). Repeat for 3 minutes.

Spinal twist: Sit in Suskasana. Grasp the shoulders with the fingers in front and thumbs at the back. Turn the torso

to the left whilst inhaling. Turn to the right whilst exhaling. Continue for 2 minutes.

Cross crawl: Lie down on your back with the arms by the sides.

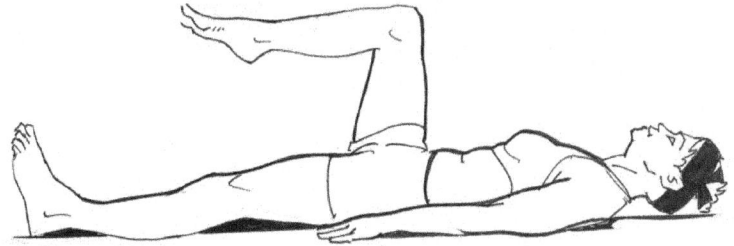

Inhale whilst bringing the left knee to the chest. Exhale whilst bringing the leg down on the floor. Repeat with the right leg. Continue for 3 minutes.

Shoulder rolls: Sit in Sukhasana. Hold your shoulders.

Roll your shoulders in big circles. Continue for 2 minutes.

Relaxation: Lie down on the floor with the arms by the sides and the eyes closed. Focus to the point between your eyebrows. Inhale and exhale deeply.

INNER SUN KRIYA
(ADVANCED IMMUNITY)

Tune in with Adi Mantra
Asana: Sukhasana
Mental Mantra: Sat Nam Wahe Guru
Mudra: Surya Mudra with left hand
Focus: on Ajna
Bandha: light Jalandhara Bandha
Pranayama: Breath of Fire
Time: 2 minutes

Cover the right nostril with the index finger of your right hand. Breathe as in the Breath of Fire. Repeat mentally the

Mantra. Start with 2 minutes and increase the interval in time to up to 5 minutes.

Mudra: Bear Mudra

Interlace the fingers with your right thumb uppermost. Breathe in and hold whilst trying to create a tension by pulling your fingers apart. Exhale. Repeat for 2 minutes.

Benefits: This Kriya increases immunity.

LAYA YOGA KRIYA FOR INTUITION

Tune in with Adi Mantra

1. **Mudra:** Left hand in Surya Mudra; right hand blocks the right nostril.
Pranayama: Breath in and out deeply
Time: 1 minute

2. **Mudra:** Right hand in Surya Mudra; left hand covers left nostril.
Pranayama: Breathe in and out deeply
Time: 1 minute

3. **Mudra:** Ego Eradicator

Pranayama: Breath of Fire
Time: 2 minutes

4. Asana: Child pose stretch
Time: 1 minute

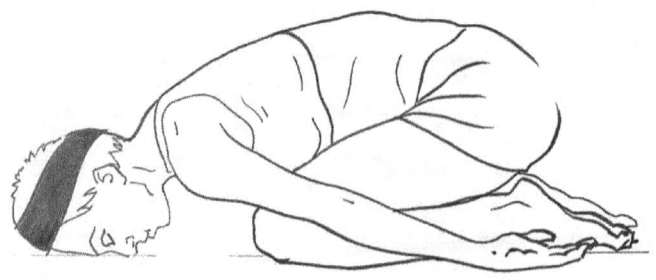

5. Mudra: Anjali Mudra above the head

Pranayama: Breathe in for 10 seconds, hold for 10 seconds, breathe out for 10 seconds
Time: 2 minutes

6. Mudra: Gyan Mudra
Bandha: Engage Mula Bandha and Jalandhara Bandha
Mantra: Ek Ong Kar Sa Ta Na Ma Siri Wahe Guru
Focus: on Ajna
Time: 11 minutes

CHAKRA CLEANSING KRIYA

Tune in with Adi Mantra

Asana: Sukhasana or Padmasana

1. **For Muladhara:** Palms on your shoulders.

Inhale and raise your arms up. Exhale and bring your palms to your shoulders. Continue for 2 minutes.

2. **For Svadhishthana:**

Legs straight in front. Hold your big toes with your fingers. Inhale and bend forward; exhale and rise back. . Continue for 2 minutes.

3. **For Manipura:** Inhale and do a right torso rotation; exhale and rotate to the left. Continue for 2 minutes.

4. **For Anahata:** Sit in Sukhasana with the palms on your shoulders.
Pranayama: Inhale and turn fast to your right; exhale and turn fast to your left.
Focus: With eyes closed, focus on the tip of your nose.
Time: 2 minutes.

5. For Vishuddha: Palms in Bear Mudra. Inhale and lift your chin. Exhale and bring the chin down. Continue for 2 minutes.

6. For Ajna: Focus on Ajna. Inhale and bring your arms up at 60 degrees with the palms in the Ego Eradicator Mudra; exhale and cover your eyes with your hands. Continue for 2 minutes.

7. **For Sahasrara:**
Asana: Sit in Sukhasana with your back straight
Mudra: Anjali Mudra.
Pranayama: Inhale deeply and swipe your aura by bringing your arms up and creating a bubble around; exhale slowly and bring your palms back to Anjali Mudra.
Focus: with your eyes closed, focus on Ajna
Time: 2 minutes.

To end: Close your eyes and breathe in and out slowly,

focusing on your breathing for 1 minute.

KUNDALINI ACTIVATION KRIYA

Tune in with Adi mantra

1. **Asana:** Sukhasana
Mudra: Ego Eradicator
Pranayama: Breath of Fire
Time: 2 minutes

2. **Asana:** Sukhasana
Mudra: Bring your arms slowly straight above your head in Venus lock Mudra; then drop them to Anjali Mudra at your chest.
Mantra: Silent Sat Nam. Mentally say *"Sat"* as you bring your arms up; mentally say *"Nam"* as you bring your arms down

Focus: With eyes closed, focus on the tip of your nose
Time: 1 minute

3. Asana: Sit in Sukhasana with palms on your knees and rotate your shoulders fast. Inhale and exhale completely.
Time: For 1 minute rotate forward, followed by 1 minute rotate backward.

4.Asana: Rock pose to Child pose for 2 minutes

Start in Rock pose

Move into Child pose

5. Asana: Archer pose
Focus: Gaze at your thumb in front
Pranayama: Breath of Fire
Time: 2 minutes on each side

5. **Asana:** Sukhasana
Mantra: Hume Hum Brahm Hum

As you chant *"Hume Hum"*, swipe your aura by bringing your arms above your head in Anjali Mudra. As you chant *"Brahm Hum"*, bring your palms back to Anjali Mudra.
Mudra: Anjali Mudra
Focus: on Ajna
Time: 11 minutes

BALANCING IDA & PINGALA KRIYA

Tune in with Adi Mantra

1. **Asana:** Sukhasana or Padmasana
Mudra: same as for the Healing Kriya
Pranayama: Inhale as you bring your left shoulder up; exhale as you bring your left shoulder down
Time: 5 minutes

2. **Asana:** Sukhasana

Cleans your aura by bringing your arms up to 60 degrees whilst inhaling. When arms are up, open wide your fingers. Exhale as you bring your arms down.
Time: 2 minutes

RADIANT BODY KRIYA

Tune in with Adi Mantra. Start moving the energy by rubbing your hands

1. **Torso rotations**
Asana: Sit in Sukhasana and start rotating clockwise for 2 minutes. Change direction for another 2 minutes.
Time: 2 minutes on both sides

2. **Asana:** Cat- Cow
Pranayama: Inhale in Cow and exhale in Cat
Time: 1 minute

3. Asana: Very fast alternate leg lifts

Time: 2 minutes

4. Asana: Cow pose to Kundalini Triangle pose
Pranayama: From Cow pose, inhale whilst pushing yourself up to the Kundalini Triangle; exhale as going back to Cow.
Time: 2 minutes

Start In Cow pose

Move into Kundalini Triangle

4. Asana: Archer pose
Pranayama: Breath of Fire
Time: 2 minutes on each side

5. **Asana:** Sukhasana. Hold your shoulders
Pranayama: inhale for 10 seconds, hold the breath for 10 seconds and exhale for 10 seconds
Time: 2 minutes

6. **Asana:** Sukhasana with arms up at 60 degrees and fingers pointing up
Pranayama: Breath of Fire
Time: 1 minute

7. **Asana:** Alternate leg raise. On your back, with your hands parallel to your body, raise fast one leg at the time

Pranayama: Inhale as you bring your leg up; exhale as you bring your leg down
Time: 2 minutes

8. **Asana:** Bend forward to one leg
Pranayama: Inhale as you bend over; exhale as you come back
Time: 2 minutes on each side

9. **Asana:** Sit with your legs straight in front of you. Hold your big toes with your fingers. Bend forward as far as you can. Keep holding your big toes. Come back to the initial position.

Pranayama: Inhale as you bend forward; exhale as you come back to sitting position.

Time: 2 minutes

10. **Asana:** Sukhasana or Padmasana, with palms holding the shoulders. Raise your arms explosively up. Bring palms back to your shoulders.

Pranayama: Inhale as your arms are reaching up; exhale as you bring your palms to your shoulders.

Time: 2 minutes

11. **Asana:** Head rotations.

As sitting in Sukhasana; start rotating your head slowly

clockwise for 1 minute; rotate anti-clockwise for another minute
Pranayama: Inhale and exhale completely
Time: 2 minutes in total

12. **Asana:** Cleanse your aura. As you sit in Sukhasana or Padmasana, bring slowly your arms up and down.
Pranayama: Inhale deeply as your arms are going up; exhale as your arms are coming down.
Time: 2 minutes

13. **Asana:** Light meditation in Rock pose with palms on your knees
Pranayama: Inhale as you chant mentally *"Sat"*; exhale as you chant mentally *"Nam"*. Focus: on Ajna
Time: 2 to 5 minutes

POWER KRIYA

Tune in with Adi Mantra

1. **Asana:** Sukhasana or Padmasana
Mudra: Bear Mudra
Bandha: engage Mula Bandha
Pranayama: Inhale for 10 seconds, hold for 10 seconds, and exhale for 10 seconds
Time: 2 minutes

2. **Asana:** Torso rotations whilst sitting in Sukhasana. Start clockwise for 1 minute; then rotate anticlockwise for 1 minute
Pranayama: Inhale for half rotation; exhale for half

3. Asana: Cobra
Time: Hold for 1 minute

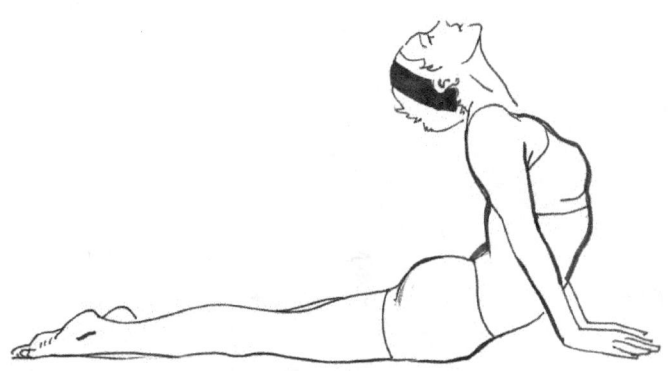

4. Asana: Sukhasana
Mudra: Ego Eradicator
Pranayama: Breath of Fire
Time: 2 minutes

5. Asana: Bend over stretch
Time: 1 minute

6. Asana: Spinal twists with palms on the shoulders. Start with turning to your right
Time: 2 minutes

7. Asana: Child pose stretch
Time: 1 minute

8. Asana: Sit in Sukhasana and bring your shoulders up.
Pranayama: Inhale as you bring your shoulders up; exhale as you drop them down.
Time: 2 minutes

9. **Asana:** Camel pose stretch (1 minute)

10. Asana: Cat- Cow
Pranayama: Inhale as you move to Cow pose; exhale as you move to Cat pose.
Time: 2 minutes

11. Asana: Sit in Sukhasana and rotate your head
Mudra: Palms on your knees
Pranayama: Inhale for half of rotation; exhale out for the other half.
Focus: on the tip of your nose
Time: 1 minute clockwise and 1 minute anticlockwise

To end: As you centre yourself, inhale and exhale slowly for 1 minute. Focus on your breathing.

CLEANSING THE 8th CHAKRA (AURA) KRIYA

Tune in with Adi Mantra

1. Asana: Sukhasana or Padmasana
Mantra: Sat Nam (long *"Sat"*; short *"Nam"*)
Mudra: Gyan Mudra
Focus: on Ajna
Time: 2 to 5 minutes

2. **Asana:** Cobra pose

Position yourself in Cobra; stay there for up to 1 minute, then release. Repeat 3 times

Pranayama: Inhale as you lift your chest up; exhale as you drop your chest down.

Time: Hold the pose each time for up to 1 minute

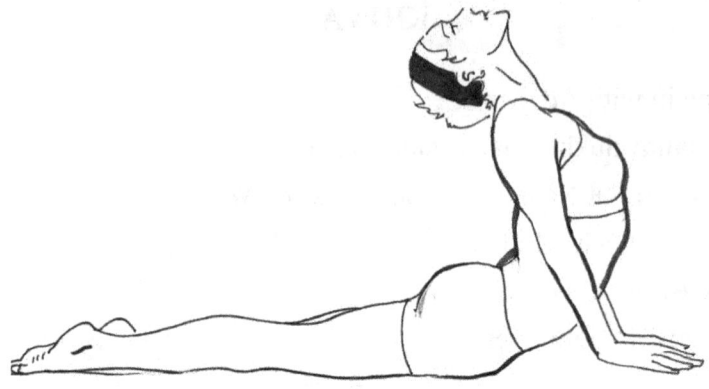

3. **Asana:** Archer pose
Pranayama: Breath of Fire
Time: 2 minutes on each side

4. **Asana:** Sukhasana or Padmasana

Bandha: Mula Bandha
Mantra: Wahe Guru, Wahe Guru, Wahe Jio
Mudra: Gyan Mudra
Time: 14 minutes

5. **Asana:** Sukhasana or Padmasana
Mantra: Sat Nam
Bring your arms above your head in Venus Lock when chanting *"Sat"*; bring your arms down at your chest in Anjali Mudra as chanting *"Nam"*.
Mudra: Anjali Mudra in front of your chest and Venus lock above the head
Time: 1 minute

AURA BALANCING KRIYA

Tune in with Adi Mantra

1. **Asana:** Sit in Sukhasana or Padmasana with the palms parallel on the floor with fingers spread. Bring your palms rapidly together in Anjali Mudra above your head.
Pranayama: Inhale as you bring your palms together; exhale as you drop them down the floor.
Time: 3 minutes

2. **Asana:** Archer pose

Pranayama: Breath of Fire
Time: 2 minute on each side

3.Asana: Cobra to Kundalini Triangle

Start in Cobra pose

Move into Kundalini Triangle

Pranayama: Inhale as you lift yourself up from Cobra to Kundalini Triangle; exhale as you come back down to Cobra.

Time: 2 minutes

4. **Asana:** Sukhasana or Padmasana

Mudra: Bear Mudra
Mantra: Wahe Guru, Wahe Jio
Time: 14 minutes

KUNDALINI FLOW KRIYA

Tune in with Adi Mantra

1. KUNDALINI IN MULADHARA

Asana: Sukhasana or Padmasana
Mudra: Anjali Mudra above the head
Pranayama: Breath of Fire
Time: 1 minute

2. RELEASE KUNDALINI FROM MULADHARA

Asana: Twist to right and left as you sit in Sukhasana or Padmasana.
Bandha: engage Mula Bandha
Time: 2 minutes

3. KUNDALINI IN SVADHISHTHANA

Asana: Sukhasana or Padmasana
Mudra: Gyan Mudra
Pranayama: Inhale for 10 seconds, hold for 10 seconds;

exhale for 10 seconds
Time: 90 seconds

4. RELEASE KUNDALINI TO MANIPURA

Asana: Sukhasana or Padmasana
Mudra: Bear Mudra (interlock your fingers)
Focus: on Ajna
Bandha: engage Mula Bandha
Time: up to 2 minutes

5. HOLD KUNDALINI IN MANIPURA

Asana: Torso rotation (clockwise) as sitting in Sukhasana. or Padmasana
Time: 2 minutes

6. RELEASE KUNDALINI TO ANAHATA

Asana: Sukhasana or Padmasana. Lift your arms above your head in Anjali Mudra; then bring them down.
Mudra: Anjali Mudra above your head
Mantra: Chant *"Sat"* as you bring your arms up; chant *"Nam"* as you bring your arms down
Time: 2 minutes. Apply Jalandhara Bandha for 20 seconds

7. HOLD KUNDALINI IN ANAHATA

Asana: Sukhasana or Padmasana

Mantra: Silent Sat Nam
Mudra: Venus Lock
Time: 3 to 5 minutes

8. RELEASE KUNDALINI TO VISHUDDHA

Asana: Head rotations whilst sitting in Sukhasana or Padmasana. Start clockwise for 1 minute. Continue anticlockwise for another minute.
Time: 2 minutes

9. RELEASE KUNDALINI TO AJNA

Bandha: engage Uddiyana Bandha for 30 seconds. Inhale and exhale deeply.

10. HOLD KUNDALINI IN AJNA

Bandha: Engage all three Bandhas: Mula Bandha, Jalandhara Bandha and Uddiyana Bandha. Inhale and exhale deeply.

11. RELEASE KUNDALINI

Asana: Sukhasana or Padmasana
Mudra: Bear Mudra (trying to pull the fingers apart)
Mantra: Ek Ong Kar Siri Wahe Guru
Time: 5 minutes

MANIPURA ACTIVATION KRIYA

Tune in with Adi Mantra

1. Asana: Alternate leg lifts
Pranayama: Inhale as you bring a leg up to 90 degrees; exhale as you bring the leg down.
Time: 5 minutes

2. Asana: Fast alternate knees to chest.
Time: 2 minutes

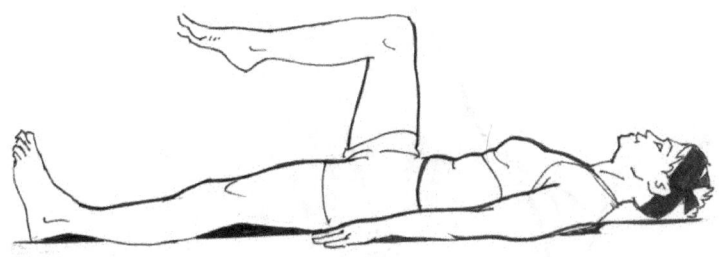

3. Asana: Bend forward as you sit with your legs straight in front.
Bandha: engage Mula Bandha
Time: 2 minutes

4. Asana: Boat pose
Time: 2 minutes

5. Asana: Bow pose
Time: 1 minute

6. Asana: Camel pose
Time: 30 seconds

7.**Asana:** Corpse pose. Lie on the back with the arms besides you. Breath in and out deeply.
Time: 2 minutes

KRIYA FOR STAMINA

Tune in with Adi Mantra

1. **Asana:** Position yourself in the Kundalini Triangle. Start moving your hips from side to side
Time: 2 minutes

2. **Asana:** Position yourself in Child Pose. Move your hands backward and interlock your fingers; bring your arms in front of your head the floor. Repeat.
Time: 3 minutes

3. **Asana:** Position yourself in Bridge pose. Drop your bottom down to just a few centimeters from the floor; come back to Bridge pose. Repeat.
Time: 3 minutes

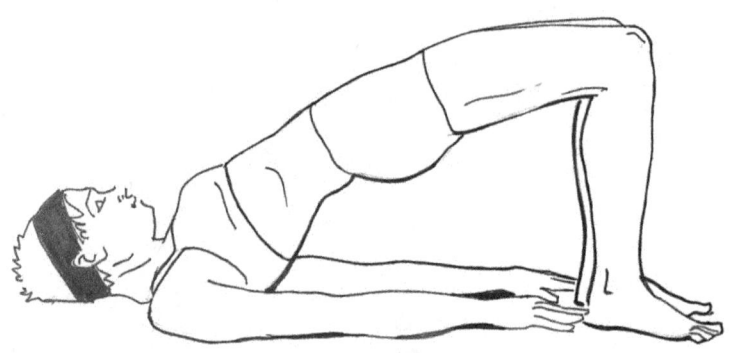

4. **Asana:** Start in Rock pose. Bend forward until your forehead touches the floor. Lift yourself up to Rock pose. Continue fast.
Time: 2 minutes

5. **Asana:** Sukhasana or Padmasana
Mudra: Venus Lock above the head
Pranayama: Breath of Fire
Time: 2 minutes

6. **Asana:** Start in Bridge pose and move to Shoulder stand pose

Pranayama: Inhale as you lift your bottom to Bridge Pose. Exhale as you bring your bottom down to the floor. Inhale as you position yourself to Shoulder stand pose.

Time: Repeat 5 times

Start in Bridge pose

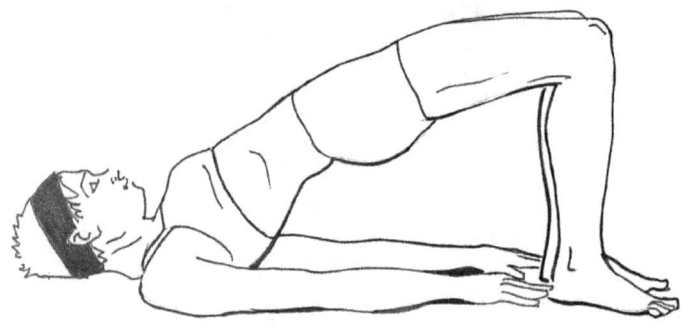

Move into Shoulder stand pose

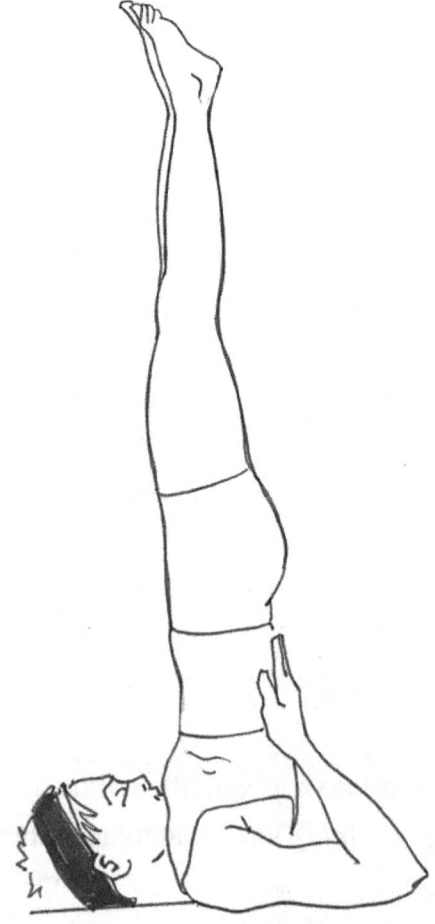

7. **Asana:** Camel pose
Time: 1 minute

8. **Asana:** Cobra to Kundalini Triangle
Pranayama: Inhale as you lift yourself up from Cobra to Kundalini Triangle; exhale as you come back to Cobra.
Time: 2 minutes

Start in Cobra

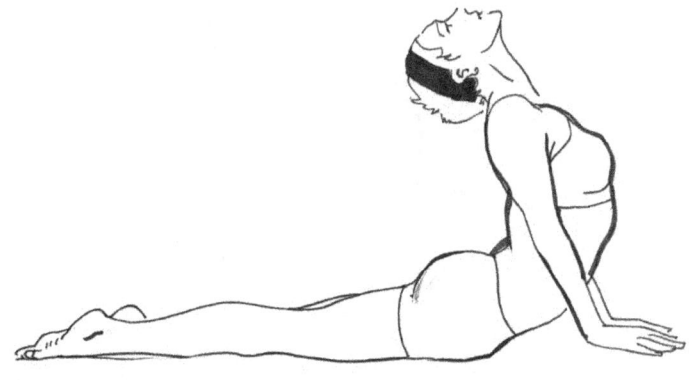

Move into Kundalini Triangle

9. **Asana:** Ego Eradicator
Pranayama: Breath of Fire
Time: 2 minutes

10. **Asana:** Sukhasana
Mudra: Anjali Mudra
Pranayama: Inhale for 10 second, hold 10 seconds; exhale for 10 seconds
Time: 2 minutes

ADVANCED MASTER KRIYAS
BACK FLEXIBILITY KRIYA

Tune in with Adi Mantra

1. Asana: In Rock Pose, with palms on your knees; flex your lower spine inward and outward
Pranayama: Inhale as you flex inward and exhale as you round your spine outward
Time: 3 minutes

2. Asana: Position yourself in wide splits and bend

forward

Pranayama: Exhale as you bend forward; inhale as you are coming back

Time: 3 minutes

3. Asana: Position yourself in Purvottanasana. Drop and raise your buttocks fast for 1 minute. Sty in Purvottanasana for another minute with Breath of Fire.

Pranayama: Breath of Fire

Time: 2 minutes in total

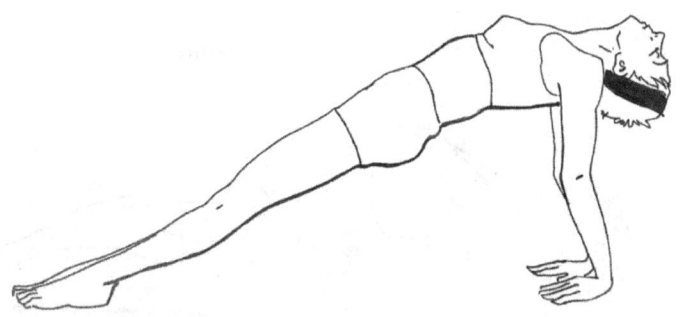

4. Asana: Position yourself in Cobra and drop your chest on the floor; then lift yourself back fast to Cobra.

Pranayama: Breath of Fire

Time: 2 minutes

5. Asana: From Rock pose to Supta Virasana pose
Pranayama: Exhale as you go backwards and inhale as you lift yourself back to Rock pose
Time: 2 minutes

Start in Rock pose

Move into Supta Virasana

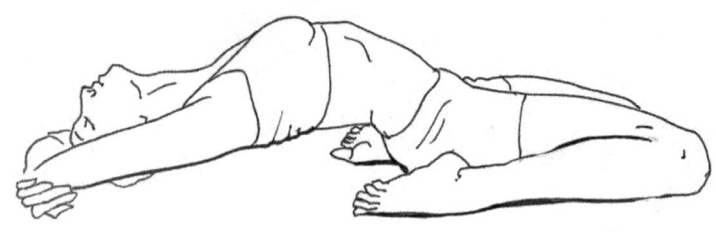

6. Asana: Sukhasana or Padmasana
Mudra: Gyan Mudra
Pranayama: Segmented breathing; one part inhale; 4 parts

exhale
Time: 2 to 3 minutes

ADVANCED MEDITATION

Tune in with Adi Mantra

Asana: Sukhasana with arms up at 60 degrees and palms wide open.
Mantra: Wahe Guru, Wahe Guru, Wahe Guru, Wahe Jio
Time: 3 to 11 minutes and another 3 to 11 minutes in Anjali Mudra, pressing your thumbs in your sternum.

To end: inhale and exhale deeply, ground yourself and open your eyes.

10 MINUTES ENERGISING KRIYA

Tune in with Adi Mantra

1. Asana: Cobra to Kundalini Triangle
Time: 2 minutes

Start with Cobra

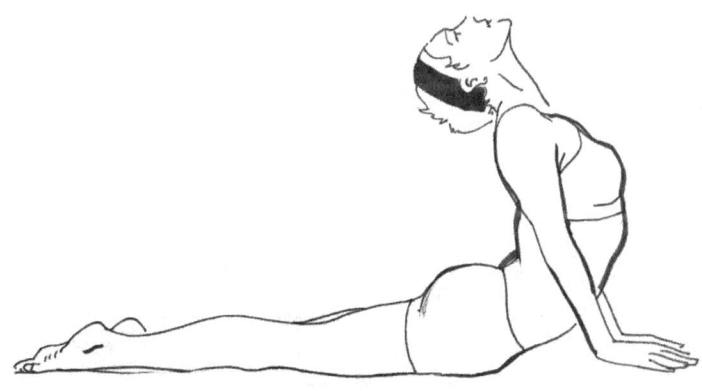

Move into Kundalini Triangle

2. Asana: Position yourself in Shoulder stand and open and close your legs. Keep the knees straight.
Time: 2 minutes

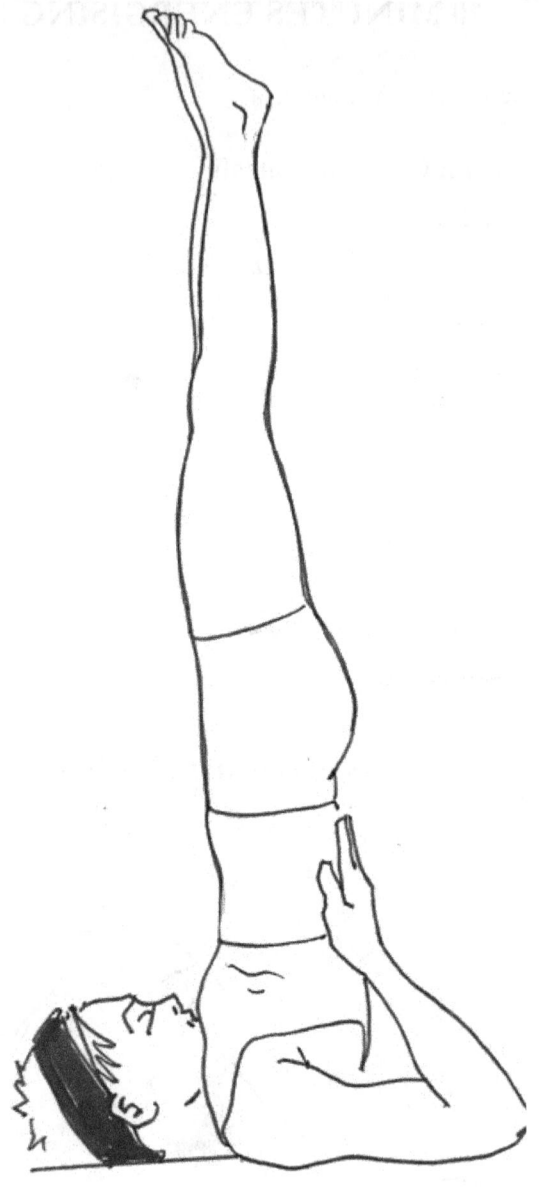

Asana: Sukhasana
Mudra: Venus Lock
Mantra: Wahe Guru
Time: 6 minutes

STRONG CORE KRIYA

Tune in with Adi Mantra

1. Asana: Very fast alternate leg lifts.
Time: 3 minutes

2. Asana: From Plow to sit with one leg straight in front pose. Start in the Plow pose. Roll fast forward by bringing one leg straight to the floor. Bend over.
Time: 2 minutes

Start in the Plow pose

Move into Bending forward pose

3. Asana: Position yourself in wide splits and bend fast forward.
Time: Continue for 2 minutes

4. Asana: Cobra
Time: 2 minutes

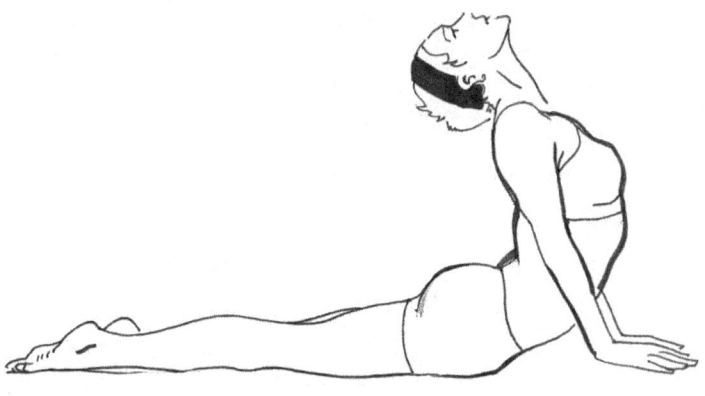

5. Asana: Crow pose
Time: up to 1 minute

6. Asana: Sukhasana or Padmasana
Mudra: Anjali Mudra above the head

Mantra: Ek Ong Kar Siri Wahe Guru
Time: 5 minutes

CHAPTER 12

NUTRITION

We, Kundalini yogis are vegetarians, but in saying that, I have to admit that vegetarianism is for some and not for others. I don't think that people should stop eating meat for no reason though. We, yogis, however have our own motives behind eating only what the soil and trees supply us with.

We base our nutrition on the Vedic philosophy, as well as on Ahimsa, one of the Yamas, part of the eight limbs of yoga[76]. Ahimsa means *"non-violence"*, so we believe that killing animals even for the sake of five star Michelin star meals is in fact nothing else than brutality. Therefore we, yogis, believe that nothing and nobody who can be a parent, in any shape or form, would be suitable for our meals. The Vedas state this very clearly referring to not killing animals: *"Do not kill those who are able to be fathers and mothers"* (Atharveda 6.140.2)

Yajurveda (1.1) teaches us to preserve life: *"Oh human! Animals are Aghnya (not to be killed). Protect the animals!"*. Therefore, from the Vedic times onwards, yogis found sources of protein in many vegetables, nuts and grains and adapted to what the Sages used to eat.

To be perfectly honest, the ban over killing animals for our meals is much deeper. All beings, human or not, are precious and we all have the same source of creation, the same atoms that interacted in the same molecules. Therefore humans and non-speaking beings have the same structure.

We believe that there is a way of protecting the planet by practicing Ahimsa and protecting life itself. The Upanishads mention that enlightenment cannot be achieved outside of non-violence. If this is the case or not, is just a matter of a personal choice. Therefore, even as a vegetarian myself, I would never suggest to anybody to give up meat because, as I have said, nutrition is a choice we all have to make based on what is good for our own bodies. We are all based on individuality and particularity even if we have a common source. Oneness doesn't mean non-diversity!

But what I would argue though is that the Western society taught us that food is everything. We work more hours than necessary only to buy more food; and because we work too much, we don't have time to cook real meals. Therefore our fridges and pantries are full of jars, boxes and plastic containers with processed foods that slowly destroy our bodies.

We socialise around food instead of enjoying each other's company. We meet our friends only to have somebody with us when we eat our meals. We eat foods that help our bodies functioning and we eat foods that destroy our bodies and it seems that these days the most developed sense is the gustatory one.

We forgot to see the beauty of our home planet, hear the sounds of nature or feel the touch of our fellow humans. Instead, we crave more and more foods and we eat them all like there is no tomorrow. We are afraid of missing out on food!

We all eat too much and we all know it. Therefore losing weight developed into one of the most profitable businesses of all. People eat more to lose more weight. As more as we eat, as fatter and unhealthier our future looks like. So, to balance it in a way or another, we swallow heaps of supplements, vitamins and minerals, forgetting that these should come from the food we eat, not from a plastic container bought at the pharmacy.

Kundalini yoga teaches to never fill the whole stomach with food; it actually says that we should always keep a third of our stomach empty. Mitahara (moderation in eating) is promoted by many Upanishads too; Shandilya[77] Upanishad calling it a real virtue. To be perfectly honest, we don't need confirmation that we overeat. We all know that we eat too much!

Food is supposed to be fuel for the body and mind; it should not be a source of pleasure. We should eat to be able to feel more alive, full of energy and stamina. We should plan our nutrition for keeping ourselves healthy, but health is the last thought we have when it is about our dinners.

If we, the twenty first century humans, want to make a change in our own wellbeing, we have to start with what we put in our guts. If we want to stop anxiety and depression spreading like a plague, we have to begin with our diet. We have to give the body the fuel it needs to function perfectly.

We, Westerners, acclaim that we want to look great, but we forget that behind that look, there is a feeling. So how would you feel if your stomach was never bloated, if your energy levels were at the maximum and if your clothes would fit perfectly? To achieve that, all you have to do is to look into your own diet. What is good it has to stay, what is bad, it shouldn't be in your pantry.

We, yogis, learnt that from our Sages. So it is not about being vegetarian or vegan. It is about what is good for each of us. For me, it is about not killing animals. I believe that life is precious and that there are so many fruits and vegetables, grains, seeds and nuts, so there is no need of killing innocent animals.

I imagine and dream about a world in which us all, humans and non-humans, can live together in harmony, without being afraid of each other. For me only, vegetarianism is a choice I made in the hope that I can contribute to that perfect world I dream about. It is also the alternative to a fit body I like to think I still have now, when I am not that young anymore.

So again, we are all different, but as more diverse we are, as more alike we become. Not when it is about food though! We all like some foods and dislike others, but what if we decide right now, in this very moment, to eat what is good for each of us, not what the advertisements in the media teach us to buy?

So make this change today. Be the master of your own body and decide for yourself what is good for you only! Take your power back, the one you gave away long time ago to media and social media, and choose to be alive!

CHAPTER 13

SADHANA

Sadhana is the yogic daily practice. Translated from Sanskrit, the term means *"the discipline to attain desired knowledge or goal"*. You cannot evolve if you are not methodical; therefore Sadhana needs repetition that in time would bring precision of your practice.

From the beginning of times, Kundalini yogis planed their practice in the ambrosial hours, the time when the sun is at sixty-degree angle to the earth. This is about one and a half hour before sunrise. We believe that the energies are stronger then and our daily spiritual practice would have a better result at that early start of the day. There are some science data behind the ambrosial hours, which imply that the planet's frequency is at that time of the day perfectly aligned with our own magnetic fields.

The Vedic texts call this time of the day Brahma Muhurta, *"God's time"* or *"the nectar time"*. The Dharmashastras, an ancient treatise on Dharma, highlights the importance of meditating in the sacred time of Brahma Muhurta.

I admit though that nowadays we are perhaps busier than our parents or grandparents were. We are always in rush from one place to another, from one activity to another, from one relationship to another... It is just the way it is. Some people love mornings; others function better at night. Therefore, the ambrosial hours are not for everybody and, if you are one of those who cannot commit to an early start, change the hours in that way that works perfectly for you.

For many years, I woke up early and started my days with my personal spiritual Sadhana. Then life took over and I had to change my time for an afternoon hour. It didn't work for me, but it may work for you. So I got back to my early spiritual practice, a few hours before the sunrise. Again, what works for me it may not be suitable for you. However, what works for everybody is never skipping a Sadhana. This is the time we allocate to meet our souls. We all have one, so we all need this date to happen every day!

I personally alternate my Kriyas during the week according to what I what to achieve, but I always finish my practice with a short meditation. I meditate again at exactly 1pm, but this time I reach for the stars.

I also chant Mantras that are relevant to me. I chant during the whole day, sometimes as an involuntary process initiated by my own mind. During the last few years, I found that the forty days chanting Sadhana worked better; since then, I decide over one Mantra, which I chant at the same time of the day for exactly forty days.

As similar our composition is, I am still not you and you are not me either. Therefore, my suggestion for those who just started on this beautiful path of Kundalini yoga is to make your own spiritual practice based on what is best for you. Pick your own times, alternate your own Kriyas and Mantras, make it all about you. As you know, we live in the Aquarian Age, so we are our own teachers. You are your best guru; never forget that!

Remember though that Sadhana means self-discipline. It is your commitment to yourself and it requires opening up to the possibility of receiving what you manifested. Let the divine energy within you guide you!

If you decide that you may give the ambrosial hours a try, always remember that thousands or maybe millions of Kundalini yogis will be there with you at the same time of the day, all meditating and keeping their bodies fit. I am one of them!

EPILOGUE

FROM A YOGI TO ANOTHER

I wished I was able to chat to you, the one who read this book, but unfortunately interaction is mostly at a virtual level these days! What in the not far past was pure face-to-face communication transformed to social media likes and followers, emails or Zoom sessions. Therefore, to you, who knows about Kundalini and attended in the past Kundalini yoga classes, I would say Sat Nam member of this huge universal family.

To you, who never been to a class, my suggestion is to try it and make your mind up only after. You may like it and, to be perfectly honest, I think that you would. Besides the beautiful songs, the love and harmony between attendants, you may find the peace you always dreamt about. You may also discover the need for synchronicity of your own soul with others out there. Oneness in all and everything is the key to save our home planet and ultimately ourselves.

If you don't believe in a higher energy, look deeper within yourself. Surprisingly or not, you may discover the holiness within yourself in a shape of an energy, implanted in you since birth… the same divine energy your local church talks about, but in a different way. Well, that energy is God!

We live in the Aquarian age and we are Aquarius children of this amazing universe. We have the power to save the world by gluing back our fragmented souls. There is no need for a mediator between us, humans and the Cosmic Soul, I refer to as God. You may call it by different names, given by your faith, science or mystical school of spirituality. You may call it Jehova, Allah, Ram Das, but at the end of the day, these are all names given by people to the same God I worship.

The good news is that this God of mine is residing in me, making me holy. The same God is manifested in you, giving you the honour and privilege to be of divine nature.

As a cohabiter of this planet, in this beautiful Aquarian Age, all you have to do is to sit back and reflect. Take the time to discover yourself and just be. Recognise that each person you look at is you packaged differently. Enjoy the symbiosis of all that is creation and be part of it in a dynamic way. Choose to love and respect yourself and others and be the blueprint of kindness.

In this beautiful Aquarian Age, nobody can talk on your behalf. You have taken the power back and you can use it in the most miraculous way to heal yourself and others. In this amazing Age, you are the master of your own destiny; you are the leader, the priest and the guru of your own faith.

The doors of heaven are open for you and everybody else on this planet and the light is brighter now than ever. If you want to find your true Self, now is the time!

We, Kundalini yogis, were taught the five main Sutras, Kundalini yoga decided on for this Aquarian Age we are all part of. We learnt to *"Recognise that the other person is you"*. We are all one in this big universe. We could all be a happy family as our Rishis prophesised or we could live as we did in the Piscean Age by ignoring everybody around and fighting hard to be on top.

If you struggle now with illness, I am addressing to you. I have been there... we all have been. This next Aquarian Age Sutra is for you: *"There is a way through every block"*. So don't despair, you will get through this and sometimes in the future, very soon though, you will look back and realise how far you have come.

If you battle financial hardship, the next Sutra is for you: *"When the time is on you, start again and the pressure will be off"*. Reach out to other people, ask for help and always remember that you are part of this huge planetary family and members of this brood are there to help. There is nothing above family!

To you all out there, I would reveal the fourth Sutra *"Understand through compassion"*. Be kind and kindness will mirror back. Understand that each and every single soul has a story you know nothing about. We all show only a small part of what happens behind our closed doors.

And finally, let me reveal the last Sutra for this glorious Aquarian Age to you all who may feel that your thoughts are louder than they should be. So if you feel that you lost your voice, don't despair and memorise this Sutra: *"Vibrate the Cosmos. The Cosmos shall clear the path"*. Raise your frequency and everything is possible. Good acts attract goodness!

Your thoughts have the power to penetrate ether, identified as the Breath of God. Inhale its breath and fill yourself in with holiness. Keep yourself anchored in the present by focusing only on your breathing. At the time we came on this planet, we were all given a number of breaths of air. Breathe in God's breath slowly and extend your time in this world and in this life.

The beginning of the Age of Aquarius may have brought tremendous events that may have shaken the whole planet, but there is nothing to fear about. Outsource your power and look to the bright future ahead!

The whole universe started with a spark of energy. Thus, if you want to be that flicker that enlightens the whole planet, have an experience of Kundalini yoga. All the Kundalini yoga teachers are taught to help you shine and, why not, pass the knowledge to you, the next teacher. I would therefore challenge and encourage you to have a taste of this beautiful style of yoga and reprogram your mind through its beautiful Kriyas.

Lastly, I will leave you all, yogis and future yogis, with the lyrics of the song all Kundalini yoga classes finish with, a blessing I would like to pass to you all. Sat Nam!

> *"May the long time sun*
> *Shine upon you.*
> *All the love surround you.*
> *And the pure light*
> *Within you*
> *Guide your way on."*

REFERENCES

1. *Staff of Osiris:* magical and powerful staff, dedicated to god Set. It enables its user to have magical power. Osiris or Usir was a primordial God in ancient Egypt. (page 3)
2. *Carl Jung* (1875- 1981) was a Swiss psychoanalyst, known for the theory of collective unconsciousness. (page 4)
3. *Yoga Upanishads* are a group of Upanishads related to the theory and practice of yoga. (page 4)
4. *Shiva*, the Destroyer, is a main deity in Hinduism, part of the Trimurti (trinity) formed by Brahma, Vishnu and Shiva. (page 4)
5. *Krishna Yajurveda* or The *"Dark"* (unarranged) Yajurveda, which has 86 Saktas (branches), is one of the two parts of Yajurveda. (page 4)
6. *Rishis* or Sages were Hindu saints (page 4)
7. *Yoni*, translated from Sanskrit at *"the womb"*, is also called Pindika (a representation of the Goddess Shakti) (page 4)
8. *Linga* or Lingam, translated from Sanskrit as *"a sign"*, is a representation of the Hindu God Shiva. (page 4)
9. *Shatkti Chalana* are powerful practices that enhance the flow of the energy in the body. (page 5)
10. *Atman* is the Self. Translated from Sanskrit is *"the soul"*. (page 5)
11. *Moksha*, also called Mukti, is the principle of freedom from the cycle of death and reincarnation. It comes from the root *"muc"* that means *"to free"*. (page 5)
12. *Samsara* is the concept of reincarnation. Translated from it Sanskrit means *"world"*. (page 5)
13. *Laya* is the concept of dissolution of self in meditation. Translated from Sanskrit it means *"withdrawal"*. (page 5)

14. *Mantra yoga* is a branch in yoga that uses Mantras to awaken the soul (page 5)
15. *Hatha yoga* is a branch in yoga, based on physicality and founded by Matsyendranath. *"Hatha"* means *"force"*. (page 5)
16. *Laya yoga* is a branch in yoga based on dissolution of selg and merge with the Supreme Consciousness. (page 5)
17. *Raja yoga* is a branch in yoga, based on mind and body control. *"Raja"* means *"King"*.
18. *Shiva Samhita* is a Sanskrit text, consisting of 5 chapters, address by Shiva to his wife Parvati. The text mentions how to practice and be successful in yoga. (page 6)
19. *Vedas* are main texts in Hinduism. There are four Vedas, Riggveda, Yajurveda, Samaveda and Atharveda, compiled by Veda Vyasa. Translated from Sanskrit, *"Veda"* or *"Vedah"* means *"knowledge"*. (page 6)
20. *Agni* is the God of Fire in Vedic mythology (page 6)
21. *Aiteraya Brahmana* is the Brahmana of the Shakala Shakta (one of the oldest Shakta or branch), part of Rigveda (page 6)
22. *Rigveda* is the oldest of the Vedas. It consists of Samhitas, Brahmanas, Aranyakas and Upanishads. It has 10 Mandalas (books), 1,28 Suktas (hymns) and 10,600 verses. (page 6)
23. *Brahmanas* are Vedic texts, transmitted orally and attached to Samhitas (mantras and hymns) (page 6)
24. *Vishnu*, the Preserver, is one of the main deities in Hinduism, part of the Trimurti (trinity) (page 7)
25. *Brahma*, the creator, is a main deity in Hinduism, part of the Trimurti (page 7)
26. *Trimurti* is the trinity in Hinduism, formed by Brahma,

Vishnu and Shiva. Their wives formed the Tridevi. (page 7)

27. *Ananta Sheshanaga* is the thousand-headed cosmic serpent in Hindu mythology, who became the bearer of the world. (page 7)

28. *Naga* is a semidivine being, half human, half serpent that can take human form. Translated from Sanskrit, *"Naga"* means *"cobra"*. (page 7)

29. *Panchikaranam* is a concept in Vedic philosophy, according to which the five elements, earth, water, fire, air and ether, are the source of creation of matter. (page 8)

30. *Saguna Brahman* is the manifested Brahman with the qualities of the Gunas. (page 8)

31. *Nirguna Brahman* is the unmanifested Brahman that is Absolute and has no qualities. (page 9)

32. *Charles Webster Leadbeater* (1854-1934) was a theosophist, author and founder of the Liberal Catholic Church. (page 10)

33. *Upanishads* are the 108 philosophical texts in the Vedas. (page 11)

34. *Agni yoga* or the *"Path to Mergence with Divine Fire"* is a theosophical religious doctrine, founded by Helena and Nicholas Roerich (page 14)

35. *Gayatri Mantra*, also known as Savitri Mantra, is Sanskrit Mantra that contains 24 letters, associated to the 24 Vedic Sages, also the 24 Devatas. Gayatri is the name of Saraswati, the wife of Brahma. (page 14)

36. *Guru Chakra*, also called Jnana Chakra, the seal of knowledge. It is part of Sahasrara structure. (page 15)

37. *Supreme Bindu* is considered the seed of the Universe. It is part of Sahasrara. (page 14)

38. *Nirvana Chakra*, part of the Sahasrara structure, is also called "The Chakra with 100 petals". It is in charge with concentration in meditation. (page 15)
39. *Ama Kala*, part of Sahasrara, is the centre in charge with experiencing Samadhi. (page 15)
40. *Nirvana Kala* is the centre where absorption with the Absolute is experience. It is part of Sahasrara structure. (page 15)
41. *Samadhi* is the highest state of mental concentration. Translated from Sanskrit it means *"total self-collectedness"*. (page 15)
42. *Chandogya Upanishad*, in the Chandogya Brahmana of the Samaveda, has eight Prapathakas (chapters). (page 18)
43. *Katha Upanishad*, also known as Kathaka Upanishad, has two Adhyayas (chapters), each with three Vallis (sections). (page 18)
44. *Lokas* are planes or realms of existence. (page 19)
45. *Kshurka Upanishad* is one of the twenty Yoga Upanishads. (page 19)
46. *Atharveda* is one of the Vedas, consisting of twenty books with 6,000 Mantras and 730 hymns. (page 19)
47. *Kula Marga*, also called the Kula Teaching, focuses on propitiation of Goddess Kulesvari. (page 21)
48. *Vedanta* is a non-dualistic school of Vedic philosophy. (page 28)
49. *Vritti* is mental awareness. (page 28)
50. *Maya* is a fundamental concept in Advaita Vedanta school of Vedic philosophy. Translated from Sanskrit, it means "Illusion". (page 28)
51. *Mandukya Upanishad,* part of Mandukya Karika in the

Rigveda, is considered a main text for Advaita Vedanta school of philosophy. (page 29)

52. *Samaveda* is one of the Vedas consisting of 1,549 verses. (page 29)
53. *Doctrine of the Three Bodies* is a concept according to which the human body consists of three bodies emanating from Brahman. (page 29)
54. *Turiya* or Chaturiya is pure consciousness. (page 30)
55. *Koshas* are energetic layers moving from the layers of skin to the spiritual core (page 30)
56. *Taittiriya Upanishad* is part of Yajurveda and has 3 Adhyayas (chapters). (page 30)
57. *Advaita Vedanta* is a monistic school of Vedic philosophy. (page 32)
58. *Maitrayenya Upanishad*, part of the Krishna Yajurveda, is formed by six Prapathakas (lessons). (page 32)
59. *Yajurveda* is one of the Vedas. It includes two parts: Krishna (black) Yajurveda and Shukla (white) Yajurveda. (page 32)
60. *Yoga Sutras of Patanjali* is a collection of Sutras (aphorisms) on the theory and practice of yoga. (page 32)
61. *Kundalini Yoga Upanishad*, also called Yogakundalini Upanishad, is one of the twenty Yoga Upanishads.
62. *Shakini* in yoga is a feminine force involved in the practice of Shiva devotion. The male equivalent is Unmatta Bhairava. Shakini appears from the body of Kuleshwar, the central deity in Yogic chakra. (page 35)
63. *Akasha* is ether from which all creation started. (page 42)
64. *Udgitha* is the chanting in the Vedic ritual; also a name for the syllable Om or the sound of the Universe. (page 43)

65. *Aitareya Brahmana* is a Brahmana in Rigveda. Aitareya Upanishad is an Upanishad in the Rigveda, based on three philosophical themes: Atman as the Universal Self, Atman undergoing threefold birth and consciousness being the essence of Atman. (page 43)
66. *Rigveda Samhita* is the most ancient layer of the Rigveda text. (page 43)
67. *Amrita*, which means *"immortality"*, is the ambrosia or the nectar of the Devas. (page 44)
68. *Ayurveda* is an ancient Indian alternative medical system. (page 44)
69. *Soma* or Amrita. See reference 67 (page 45)
70. *Guru Granth Sahib* is the central holy scripture of Sikhism. (page 47)
71. *Sikhism* is a philosophy and religion in India, established by Guru Nanak (1469- 1539). (page 47)
72. *Pancha Boota* is the concept of the five elements, earth, wind, fire, water and ether, which are the base of the cosmic creation. (page 58)
73. *Brahmins* are the highest caste of priests. (page 59)
74. *Yogi Bhajan* (Harbhajan Singh Kalsa) 1929-2004 was a Sikh who brought Kundalini yoga to the Western world. (page 69)
75. *Vratyas* were pre Vedic tribes migrating through the North East India (page 182)
76. *The eight limbs of yoga* are: Yamas (attitude toward environment), Niyama (attitude toward ourselves), Asana (postures), Pranayama (breathing techniques), Dharana (concentration), Dhyana (meditation), and Samadhi (complete integration). The 5 Yamas are: Ahimsa (non-

violence), Satya (truthfulness), Asteya (non-stealing), Brachmacharya (continence), Aparigraha (noncovetousness). The 5 Nyanas are: Soucha (cleanliness), Samtosa (contentment), Tapas (spiritual austerities), Svadhyaya (study of the scriptures) and Isvara Pranidana (surrender to God). (page 182)

77. *Shandilya Upanishad* is one of the twenty Yoga Upanishads. (page 184)

ABOUT THE AUTHOR

Brigitte Calloway is a Clinical Hypnotherapist, who runs a busy practice in Inglewood, New Zealand. She teaches workshops on the subjects of astral projection, karma, past life regression, meditation, energy systems and vibration.

After hours, she enjoys playing drums, bass guitar, Indian harmonium and spending time with her dog Hendrix. She has a passion for growing and propagating orchids.

Brigitte is a Kundalini yogi. She is a published author of three books: *"You have lived many times"*, *"We have met in past lives"* and *"Kabbalah and Vedic wonderings"*.

www.ingramcontent.com/pod-product-compliance
Lightning Source LLC
Chambersburg PA
CBHW060512090426
42735CB00011B/2192